Unit 3

HISTORY & GEOGRAPHY 803
The American Revolution (1763–1789)

INTRODUCTION |3

1. GROWING CONFLICT 5

BRITAIN FLEXES ITS MUSCLES |6
ACTIONS AND REACTIONS |11
REBELLION |16
SELF TEST 1 |27

2. WAR 31

AMERICA ALONE |31
THE TURNING POINT |39
THE END OF THE WAR |45
SELF TEST 2 |51

3. THE CONSTITUTION 55

THE ARTICLES OF CONFEDERATION |56
CONSTITUTIONAL CONVENTION |60
THE BATTLE OF RATIFICATION |64
SELF TEST 3 |68

LIFEPAC Test is located at the back of the booklet. Please remove before starting the unit.

The American Revolution (1763–1789) | Unit 3

Author:
Theresa Buskey, B.A., J.D.

Editor:
Alan Christopherson, M.S.

Westover Studios Design Team:
Phillip Pettet, Creative Lead
Teresa Davis, DTP Lead
Nick Castro
Andi Graham
Jerry Wingo

804 N. 2nd Ave. E.
Rock Rapids, IA 51246-1759

© MCMXCIX by Alpha Omega Publications, Inc. All rights reserved. LIFEPAC is a registeredtrademark of Alpha Omega Publications, Inc.

All trademarks and/or service marks referenced in this material are the property of their respective owners. Alpha Omega Publications, Inc. makes no claim of ownership to any trademarks and/or service marks other than their own and their affiliates, and makes no claim of affiliation to any companies whose trademarks may be listed in this material, other than their own.

Unit 3 | **The American Revolution (1763–1789)**

The American Revolution (1763–1789)

Introduction

The struggle for independence by the United States has often baffled historians. Raw courage and determination in many cases were the only resources the colonists had to depend upon. The American government during the war was ineffective and disorganized. The army lacked basic supplies and regular soldiers. Yet, these raw colonials defeated the greatest military power of their era, Great Britain.

Historians have also long debated the reasons for the war. At the end of the French and Indian War, the American colonies were joyfully, deeply British. No one dreamed in 1763 that there would be a war between the colonies and Britain just twelve years later. Those years were a litany of miscalculations on the part of Britain that drove the colonists further and further from the loyalty of 1763.

This LIFEPAC® will discuss the events that caused the Revolution. It will also present a history of the Revolution itself, the major battles, ideas, and events. Finally, this LIFEPAC will show how the colonists finally managed to create a stable government under the United States Constitution.

Objectives

Read these objectives. The objectives tell you what you will be able to do when you have successfully completed this LIFEPAC. When you have finished this LIFEPAC, you should be able to:

1. Identify the men who contributed to the Revolution.
2. Identify and describe the incidents and thinking which led to the Revolution.
3. Identify and describe the governing bodies that acted for the colonies/states.
4. Name the major battles of the war and tell their significances.
5. Outline the terms of the peace agreements that the United States signed with Great Britain.
6. Explain the Articles of Confederation and why they were replaced.
7. Describe the Constitutional Convention.
8. Describe the main features of the Constitution and the process by which it was approved.

The American Revolution (1763–1789) | Unit 3

Survey the LIFEPAC. Ask yourself some questions about this study and write your questions here.

1. GROWING CONFLICT

The American colonists were delighted with the outcome of the French and Indian War. The hated French had finally been driven out of their land. They were free to expand into the rich lands of the eastern Mississippi basin. They were proud to be British, part of the mighty British Empire.

But, even in the midst of the joy, the first signs of the difference between the colonists and the government in Britain appeared, the Proclamation of 1763. The king tried to block the colonists behind the Appalachian Mountains, but the colonists chose to ignore the order. Worse was to come.

In the years that followed, the British tried to tax and control the colonies for the first time in colonial history. The Sugar Act, the Stamp Act, the Townshend Acts, and the Intolerable Acts beat a steady path to rebellion in the colonies. The colonists saw a conspiracy to deprive them of their liberty and reacted with resistance. The British saw no valid reason for the increasing resistance to their "lawful" decrees and reacted with more force. Finally, the colonists gave up hope of a peaceful settlement and chose to fight rather than submit.

SECTION OBJECTIVES

Review these objectives. When you have completed this section, you should be able to:

1. Identify the men who contributed to the Revolution.
2. Identify and describe the incidents and thinking which led to the Revolution.
3. Identify and describe the governing bodies that acted for the colonies/states.

VOCABULARY

Study these words to enhance your learning success in this section.

arbitrary (är′ bi trer′ ē). Not going by any rule or law.
conservative (kon sėr′ va tiv). A person who is opposed to change.
militia (mu lish′ a). Army of citizens who are not regular soldiers.
moderate (mod′ er it). A person whose political views are not extreme in any way.
Prime Minister (prīm′ min′ i stir). The chief official in certain types of government.
propaganda (prop′ a gan′ da). Systematic efforts to spread opinions or beliefs.
protocol (prō′ tu kol). Rules (written or unwritten) for a procedure.
providential (prov′ u den′ shul). Good fortune happening by God's intervention (the Christian version of "good luck"-author).
radical (rad′ i kal). A person who favors extreme changes or reform.

Note: *All vocabulary words in this LIFEPAC appear in* **boldface** *print the first time they are used. If you are not sure of the meaning when you are reading, study the definitions given.*

Pronunciation Key: hat, āge, cãre, fär; let, ēqual, tėrm; it, īce; hot, ōpen, ôrder; oil; out; cup, pu̇t, rüle; child; long; thin; /ϮH/ for then; /zh/ for measure; /u/ or /ə/ represents /a/ in about, /e/ in taken, /i/ in pencil, /o/ in lemon, and /u/ in circus.

The American Revolution (1763–1789) | Unit 3

Britain Flexes its Muscles

British attitudes. Britain was the greatest power on earth after the Seven Years (French and Indian) War. It had soundly defeated its great rival, France, and taken her North American empire. The British were proud and arrogant about their victory. They were confident of their own glory and were not in a mood to compromise with anyone, especially their backwoods colonies.

Moreover, the war had left Britain deeply in debt. The national debt had doubled and the new territory in America would be expensive to administer. Pontiac's War was launched by Native American tribes in the Great Lakes region, proving that the British needed to maintain troops in the colonies for their protection. That was expensive. The government felt it was high time the colonists bore some of the cost of their own defense.

Mercantilism. The popular economic theory of the 1700s was mercantilism. This theory held that only gold or silver was real wealth, and countries must work to obtain more of it. Colonies were used to doing this through trade. Colonies were to supply the mother country with raw materials such as wood, iron, and indigo. Then, the colonies would be a market for goods manufactured by the mother country, like cloth, hats, and tools. The colony was not to compete with the mother country by building its own manufacturing and industry. This theory held that the colony only existed to serve the mother country and should never be allowed to develop. It should be kept dependent on the mother country at all times.

British policy towards America was based on mercantilism. The Navigation Acts, which were passed mainly in the late 1600s, were intended to force the colonies to act in accord with this theory. One of the laws required that all trade with the colonies had to be on English or colonial ships.

| The American British Empire in 1763

Another required all colonial trade to go through England to be taxed. That meant that goods going from the colonies to the French West Indies, just south of Florida, had to go to England, be unloaded, stored, and taxed before they could go to their destination. The same was true in reverse for goods coming from the West Indies or Europe to the colonies. This gave English merchants a virtual monopoly on colonial trade, because the cost of going through England made foreign trade too expensive. Other laws stated that certain important goods like tobacco and naval supplies could only be sold to Britain, even if Britain could not possibly buy all that the colonies could produce. These laws would have crippled colonial trade, but until 1763 they were rarely enforced, and the colonists traded with many nations by smuggling.

There were other laws on the books by 1763 that were intended to keep the colonies economically backward and dependent on Britain. The colonies were forbidden to export wool cloth, hats or tools. They were also forbidden to build iron mills to make tools. The Molasses Act of 1733 put a high tax on molasses, sugar, and rum imported from non-British sources, primarily the French West Indies. The problem was that the British West Indies could not supply half of the molasses needed by the distilleries in New England. (The molasses was made into rum for sale at home and abroad). So, the law was routinely and easily avoided by smuggling.

One of the more damaging laws forbade the colonies to mint coins. British merchants could not pay for colonial products in hard money (coins). That meant the colonies were always short of coins they needed to pay for British goods. It also made it difficult for colonists to collect enough money to start any large businesses. The colonists had to barter for most of their goods and try to get coins by trade with French and Spanish lands. These restrictions were very unpopular in the colonies, but, obviously, very popular in London.

| George III, King of England

Changes in policy. After the Seven Years War, Britain began to change her policy toward the colonies. The British government had been content for over a hundred and fifty years to let the colonies govern themselves. Now, flush with pride in their victory, they felt it was time for Parliament to establish better control over the empire. There was also a strong feeling that since the British had spent both blood and treasure to protect the colonies, the colonies owed them something in return. What the British expected to get was loyalty and some income to help defray the huge costs of stationing troops in America.

George Grenville became **Prime Minister** of Great Britain in 1763. He moved quickly to meet the new mood of the king, George III, and Parliament. He began in 1763 by ordering that the Navigation Acts be strictly enforced. He obtained the Sugar Act of 1764 from the Parliament that decreased the high tax on French molasses but kept high taxes on sugar and rum. He arranged for this act to actually be enforced by customs offices and an Admiralty Court.

The American Revolution (1763–1789) | Unit 3

That court did not use a jury and the defendant was assumed to be guilty, not innocent as in regular courts. The colonists saw this as a threat to their English liberties. The next law was a Quartering Act in 1765 that required colonists to provide food and lodging for British troops. These acts angered the Americans, but it was the next one that set fire to the dynamite, the Stamp Act.

| An early U.S. Flag

 Answer these questions.

1.1 What was the popular economic theory of the 1700s?
_____

1.2 According to that theory what should a colony do for a mother country?
_____
_____

1.3 What were the goals of the British government toward the colonies in 1763?
   a. _____
   b. _____

1.4 What were the major parts of the Navigation Acts?
   a. _____
   b. _____
   c. _____

1.5 What was the Molasses Act of 1733? Why would it have hurt the New England colonies and why didn't it? _____
_____
_____

1.6 Why were the colonies short of hard money? _____
_____

1.7 What did George Grenville do to anger the colonies in
   1763? _____
   1764? _____
   1765? _____

8 | Section 1

The Stamp Act. Grenville proposed to raise a substantial amount of money in the colonies by the Stamp Act, passed in 1765. The law required all legal documents and public papers, such as wills, playing cards, newspapers, and bills of sale, to be marked with a stamp purchased from the government. Grenville thought this was a reasonable way to raise money. The amount charged for the stamps would be less than a similar stamp in Britain and the money would be used to pay British troops in the colonies. Even Benjamin Franklin, the colonial representative in London, who disapproved of the law expected the colonists to accept it after a few protests.

However, the Stamp Act was seen as a threat in America. It was the first time Britain had tried to directly tax the colonists. Taxes before had been on imports and were intended mostly to control trade. Any other taxes had only come from the colonial assemblies elected by the colonists. The tax fell on everyone from the card playing sailors to wealthy merchants or lawyers whose trade depended on documents. Moreover, the colonists were constantly short of the money needed to buy the stamps. Even worse, people who violated the act were to be tried in Admiralty Courts! The colonists thought Britain was trying to reduce them and set them up for failure with all these new laws.

It was the very visible Stamp Act that drew the wrath of the colonists, who were united in their opposition to it. The Americans said Parliament could not tax them, since there were no American representatives in Parliament. The battle cry that would open the Revolution was: "No taxation without representation." But, more than shouting slogans, the Americans began to organize, unite, and resist. This was the real legacy of the Stamp Act.

The controversy was a repeat of the conflict between Parliament and the king in England. The Glorious Revolution (1688) had established that political power in England would be in the hands of an elected body, Parliament, not an autocratic king. The colonists felt that if they indeed had the rights of Englishmen, then the political power in their land should be in the hands of their representatives. The British Parliament could not step in as a new monarch to rob the colonists of their traditional English liberties. Parliament thought of the colonists as subjects who should obey, not as citizens who should participate. This arrogant attitude was intolerable.

| Patrick Henry

The House of Burgesses in Virginia debated and passed the Virginia Resolves, which declared the act illegal, stating that only Virginians could tax Virginians. The debate over the Resolves included a famous speech by **radical** member Patrick Henry. He said, "Caesar had his Brutus–Charles the First, his Cromwell–and George the Third–may profit by their example." When the **conservative** members of the Burgesses began to whisper, "Treason," Henry replied, "If this be treason, make the most of it."

The reaction to the Stamp Act came in three major ways: the Stamp Act Congress, boycotts, and mob action. The Massachusetts assembly invited all the colonies to send delegates to New York to discuss the Stamp Act.

Nine of the colonies sent delegates to what became known as the Stamp Act Congress. The delegates were wealthy, distinguished men from the elite of the colonies. They passed a Declaration of Rights and Grievances stating that only the colonies could tax their own citizens. Britain ignored it. It was, however, a significant step in uniting the colonies, most of which thought of themselves almost as separate nations.

A much more effective message was sent to Parliament when the colonies began to boycott British goods. They were very successful in organizing agreements not to import British products. Colonists found other sources to meet their needs, or self-sufficiently went without them. The boycott began to threaten the prosperity of the English merchants who complained to Parliament. Parliament listened.

The last way that the colonists resisted the Stamp Act was by mob action, this was also very effective. The "Sons of Liberty," secret societies opposed to the act, took the law into their own hands. They attacked stamp sellers, royal officials, and people who violated the boycott. On the date the law was to take effect, November 1, 1765, there were no officials to sell the hated stamps. All had resigned in fear of the mobs.

Faced with an outcry in Britain and the colonies, and knowing they were not collecting any revenue, Parliament repealed the Stamp Act four months after it went into effect. At the same time they passed the face-saving Declaratory Act, stating that Parliament had the right to tax the colonies. The colonists rejoiced at their victory and, with a few exceptions, ignored the dark implications of the Declaratory Act. They had acted together, sometimes with violence, and accomplished what they wanted. The lesson would be remembered.

Name the requested item or person.

1.8 British Prime Minister who passed the Stamp Act
_____

1.9 Colonial representative in London who thought the Act would be obeyed
_____

1.10 Radical in House of Burgesses who said, "If this be treason, make the most of it."
_____

1.11 Burgesses statement against the Stamp Act
_____

1.12 Three ways the colonies reacted to the Stamp Act

a. _____

b. _____

c. _____

1.13 Secret societies that led mob action against the Stamp Act
_____

1.14 The slogan against the tax

_____

1.15 Law stating that Parliament had a right to tax the colonies

_____

Answer these questions.

1.16 What did the Stamp Act require?

_____

_____

1.17 Why did the colonists object so much to it? (four reasons)

_____

_____

1.18 What did Patrick Henry mean in his speech about Brutus and Cromwell? (Look up the named people if you need to.)

_____

_____

Actions and Reactions

Townshend Acts. The failure of the Stamp Act did not help Britain's financial problems. The debt remained along with the huge expense of protecting North America. The king and the powerful people in Britain were furious. They wanted the rebellious colonies brought in line. Finally, Britain had another change in government (this happened frequently). The new Chancellor of the Exchequer (Treasury), Charles Townshend promised to pluck the colonial goose with a minimum of squawking.

Townshend succeeded in passing a series of laws through Parliament in 1767. Called the Townshend Acts, they were designed to increase revenue and control. The most important put a tax on a large number of goods such as paint, lead, glass, paper, and tea that the colonies imported from Britain. This was an indirect tax which Townshend thought the colonies would accept.

Another act greatly increased the power of customs officials to enforce the tax laws, including the use of writs of assistance which allowed **arbitrary** searches of homes and businesses. Another law threatened to shut down the New York assembly if it did not comply with the Quartering Act (it had refused up until that point). Moreover, the money raised was to be used to pay British officials, including governors, in the colonies. This meant the colonists could no longer hope to control royal officials by limiting their salary!

The colonists were alarmed. They had fought with royal governors often enough to know the loss of the power of the purse would leave them helpless against arbitrary rule. They also saw the strict enforcement procedures as a violation of the basic legal rights of all Englishmen. The threat to suspend the New York legislature threatened every assembly in the colonies.

The uneasy colonists began to believe there was a conspiracy afoot to take away their rights. The taxes themselves, however, did not create the unanimous outcry of the Stamp Act. They were subtle and indirect, but still not acceptable.

The colonists objected to the Townshend Acts, but the reactions were not as strong or as quick as under the Stamp Act. Radicals like Samuel Adams from Boston wrote pamphlets urging action. John Dickinson, a lawyer and legislator, wrote a series of widely read articles called *Letters from a Farmer in Pennsylvania*, which argued that the Parliament had no power over colonial affairs. Several colonial assemblies were dissolved for supporting that idea. A boycott was slowly pulled together. The colonists also engaged in widespread smuggling to bring in products and avoid paying the taxes.

Boston Massacre. Massachusetts, founded by independent-minded Puritans, had always been a restive colony. Boston quickly became a center for the opposition to Britain. The Sons of Liberty were especially active there, interfering with the British officials and creating public disturbances. Finally, the government sent in British soldiers to keep order. The presence of soldiers in the midst of an angry population was asking for trouble, and it came.

On the evening of March 5, 1770, a crowd decided to entertain themselves by throwing snowballs at a soldier guarding the Customs House. Troops were sent to his aid. The crowd threw snowballs and debris at them. Despite the efforts of Captain Preston, the commander, to prevent it, someone opened fire on the mob. Five people were killed. The colonial **propaganda** called the incident the Boston Massacre.

Radicals spread the news all through the colonies. The public story made martyrs out of the dead. The soldiers involved were tried for murder. John Adams, patriot and future president, took the unpopular job of defending them. He did so well that only two were convicted and those received light sentences. The results added to colonial distrust and anger.

| The Boston Massacre

Repeal. In Britain, the boycotts slowly began to have some effect on commerce. Thanks in part to colonial interference, the taxes were bringing in very little money. Moreover, the British government realized it was foolish to tax their own goods they were trying to sell in America. Lord North, who was now in control of the government, repealed the taxes in 1770, except for the tax on tea. The king and others insisted it must remain as a symbol of the government's right to tax.

The repeal calmed the **moderates** and relieved the conservatives, but radicals still looked for a confrontation with the British. Samuel Adams of Boston took the lead in organizing groups to communicate between the towns in Massachusetts. These *Committees of Correspondence* were set up to exchange information and the latest news. They also kept the rebellious spirit active. Eventually, they were set up by all the colonies to communicate with each other, laying the foundation for future cooperation.

Unit 3 | **The American Revolution (1763–1789)**

 Answer true or false.

If the statement is false, change some of the nouns or adjectives to make it true.

1.19 _____ The Townshend duties taxed goods imported from France.

1.20 _____ Charles Townshend was the Prime Minister.

1.21 _____ Money from the Townshend taxes was to be used to pay British officials in the colonies.

1.22 _____ The Townshend Acts threatened to dissolve the Massachusetts assembly if it did not comply with the Stamp Act.

1.23 _____ The colonists did not react as fiercely to the Townshend Acts as they had to the Stamp Act.

1.24 _____ *Letters from a Farmer in Pennsylvania* argued that colonial assemblies had no power over affairs in the colonies.

1.25 _____ The Townshend Acts were also met with a boycott.

1.26 _____ Lord West repealed all of the Townshend duties except the tax on paint.

1.27 _____ Committees of Correspondence encouraged communication and cooperation between the colonies.

1.28 _____ Britain was deeply in debt and was paying to protect America.

Describe the following.

1.29 The Townshend Acts

_____
_____
_____
_____

1.30 The Boston Massacre

_____
_____
_____
_____

Boston Tea Party. In 1773, the British East India Company was in serious financial trouble. Lord North decided to help it by giving it a monopoly on the sale of tea to the American colonies. The prices were set so that, even with the tax, it was cheaper than tea smuggled in from other sources. The colonists distrusted the monopoly and saw the lower price as a way to sneak the tax by them. They made sure that none of the tea was ever sold in America.

The colonies reacted differently to the tea when it arrived. Pennsylvania stuck it in a warehouse to rot. Charleston also stored it, and later sold it to support the Revolution. But, it was the reaction of the Sons of Liberty in Boston that gained the most fame. Three tea ships were floating in Boston harbor on the night of December 16, 1773. None had been able to unload their cargo. That evening a group of colonists, thinly disguised as Native American people, boarded the ships, took the tea, and dumped it into the harbor. The entire protest, known as the Boston Tea Party, was orderly and completely without violence. They simply refused to accept the tea. The tea party was repeated in New York harbor by a group of patriots there.

The Intolerable Acts. The reaction in London to the Tea Party was one of uncontrolled fury. The public destruction of valuable property in defiance of the king was the last straw. Public opinion was united behind Lord North and the king as they decided that Boston must be brought to heel. A series of laws called the Coercive Acts in Britain, and the Intolerable Acts in America were rapidly passed by Parliament.

The most important of the Intolerable Acts was the Boston Port Bill. It ordered the port of Boston blockaded and closed until the tea was paid for, with the tax. The implication of this was staggering. The closing of the harbor would mean the destruction of the city which depended on commerce for its supplies, jobs, and revenue. An entire city was being destroyed for the non-violent actions of a few individuals, clearly an excessive and dangerous use of force.

The other parts of the Intolerable Acts were equally as odious. The Massachusetts charter was changed so that all important officials were appointed and controlled by the Crown. Town meetings were forbidden without the express approval of the governor. A military governor was appointed for Boston and more troops were sent in, putting it under military rule.

The British government expected the other colonies to see this as a matter only involving Boston and stay out of it. They expected other port cities to jump at the chance to take over some of Boston's trade. In fact, the other colonies did not see it that way. They realized that if Britain could successfully use that kind of force against Boston, it would likely be used later against other colonies. They acted, therefore, in support of Boston, sending supplies to the city by land from as far away as South Carolina.

Quebec Act. Passed with the Intolerable Acts in Britain was a piece of legislation called the Quebec Act. It was not a part of the laws aimed at the colonies, but the touchy Americans assumed it was. The law confirmed the rights of the French in Quebec to follow their own customs (which did not include the usual traditions of English liberty) and protected the Catholic religion. Moreover, it extended the boundaries of Quebec down into the Ohio Valley south of the Great Lakes. That cut the Americans off from any possibility of controlling that coveted land, and put the land under a foreign system of government. The Quebec Act was a wise attempt by Parliament to win the support of the citizens in the former French lands. The Americans saw it as a spread of hated Catholicism, and a further attempt to contain their liberties.

Unit 3 | **The American Revolution (1763–1789)**

The First Continental Congress. The primary response to the Intolerable Acts was the First Continental Congress. The colonies realized they needed to act together. Using the Committees of Correspondence, they set up a meeting for September 1774 in Philadelphia. Every colony except Georgia sent delegates. The fifty-four delegates included Samuel and John Adams from Massachusetts, John Jay from New York, as well as George Washington and Patrick Henry from Virginia.

The Congress accomplished several things during the seven weeks it met. They passed a Declaration of Rights that included life, liberty, property, the right to assemble and to tax themselves. Several acts of Parliament were declared to be illegal and an Association was formed to enforce a *full stoppage* of trade until the acts were repealed. A petition was sent to the king to address the colonial complaints.

| The First Continental Congress

The Congress further agreed to meet again in May of 1775 if their demands had not been met by then.

Choose the correct word(s) to complete these sentences.

1.31 Lord North gave the _____ a monopoly on the sale of tea to America to in 1773.

1.32 The tea that was shipped to the city of _____ was stored and later sold to support the Revolution.

1.33 A second tea party occurred in the city of _____ after the one at Boston.

1.34 The _____ Bill closed Boston harbor until the tea and tax were paid for.

1.35 The _____ Act protected the traditional customs of the French in Quebec and expanded their territory.

1.36 The primary colonial response to the Intolerable Acts was to organize the _____ _____ .

1.37 The Intolerable Acts were the British reaction to the _____ .

Describe the following.

1.38 The Intolerable Acts

_____

_____

_____

1.39 The Boston Tea Party

_____

_____

_____

1.40 The actions of the First Continental Congress

_____

_____

_____

1.41 The American view of the Quebec Act

_____

_____

_____

Rebellion

Lexington and Concord. All of the American colonies had **militias** in the 1700s. They had been been organized to protect the colonists from the Native Americans and the French. In the wake of the occupation of Boston, the militias began to drill and collect supplies to defend themselves against British troops. The Massachusetts assembly, which had been meeting illegally, chose the city of Concord as a major supply depot for the militia. The assembly also began meeting there to be out of the reach of General Gage, the military commander of Boston.

Gage found out about the supplies and decided to destroy them. He also hoped to arrest some of the colonial leaders such as Samuel Adams and John Hancock, who were staying in Lexington. In April of 1775, Gage sent over 700 men to Lexington during the night. Paul Revere, a Boston silversmith who had worked for many years as a courier for the Sons of Liberty, rode to warn the patriots. In accordance with plans laid in advance, two lights were put in the steeple of the Old North Church to let the patriots know that the soldiers were coming across the Charles River. Revere only made it as far as Lexington before he was captured by a British patrol. But, other riders brought word to Concord.

When the British arrived at Lexington on the morning of April 19th, they were met by two companies of militia drawn up in battle order.

Battle order in the 1700s was two lines of men, one behind the other, close together. This was the standard because of the type of weapon they used, muskets. Muskets were very inaccurate and could not be counted on to hit a target more than 100 yards away. The only way to be sure of hitting anything was to have a large mass of men, firing together at the target at close range. Military **protocol** required that this be done on an open field until one side withdrew leaving the victors in command of the field.

The American commander realized that he was heavily outnumbered. When he was ordered to disperse, he began to do so. As the Americans began to leave, someone fired a shot. That bullet has been called "The Shot Heard Around the World" because it started the Revolutionary War. When the British officers finally got their men back under control, eight Americans were dead.

The British went on to Concord where they destroyed some supplies. There, they confronted a larger militia force who forced them to retreat. The retreat quickly became dangerous. The Americans, contrary to all the rules of gentlemanly warfare, began firing at the soldiers from behind trees, rocks, and buildings as they withdrew. The arrival of reinforcements at Lexington kept the British from being destroyed. Even then, it was a long march back to Boston as the militia opened fire from any vantage point they could find all along the route back. In the end, about seventy British soldiers were killed. America was at war with Britain.

Capture of Lake Champlain. Roads in the colonies were terrible. The best and most reliable transportation was by water. In central New York, there was a key water route that almost bridged the gap between Canada and the Atlantic coast. The Riechelieu River connected the St. Lawrence with Lake Champlain. The southern end of the lake was only 23 miles from the Hudson River, which flowed through Albany to New York City. This key route was protected by two old forts, Ticonderoga and Crown Point. Both forts were taken by a New England force under Ethan Allen and Benedict Arnold in May of 1775, to protect New England from a Canadian-based invasion. The forts were in bad shape, but Ticonderoga had a large supply of good cannon, something the colonists needed. Henry Knox, who would eventually become the first Secretary of War, went to Ticonderoga to get them. In the dead of winter in 1775-76, he moved 59 cannons across miles of wilderness to give the British a nasty surprise.

Bunker Hill. Militia from all over New England began to gather around Boston after Lexington and Concord. The slowly assembling citizen's army was put under the command of Artemas Ward of Massachusetts. Ward decided to fortify Bunker Hill on the Charlestown Peninsula facing Boston. By mistake, his men put up their fortifications on nearby Breeds Hill, but the battle that followed was named for the place where it should have happened.

The British foolishly decided to make a frontal attack on the entrenched, protected Americans at the top of the hill. They probably believed that the amateurs would run at the first sight of a regular army. The Americans did not bring enough gunpowder with them for a long battle, but they were determined to stay.

On June 17, 1775, about 2,000 British soldiers in neat lines marched up the hill toward the Americans. The militia calmly waited and held their fire until they "could see the whites of their eyes." Then, the Americans opened fire, mowing down the unprotected "Redcoats." The British retreated and came again, with the same result. The Americans held until they ran out of gunpowder and then managed to retreat. The British had lost almost half of their men, dead or wounded. Even though the British took the hill, the heavy losses made it more of an American victory. One colonial leader commented that he would gladly sell the British another hill at the same price.

The American Revolution (1763–1789) | Unit 3

A Colonial army. The Second Continental Congress assembled in May of 1775 as they had arranged. This time all thirteen colonies were represented, and Benjamin Franklin, newly returned from London, was a Pennsylvania delegate. The Congress at that time still did not want independence, nor did most of the country. They saw the fighting more as a civil war in defense of their rights. Congress, however, agreed to take on the assembling forces around Boston as an *American* army and to appoint a commander-in-chief. They chose George Washington for the post. It was a **providential** choice.

Washington was the son of a wealthy Virginia planter and had increased his fortune by marrying a rich widow, Martha Custis. He had been a colonial officer in the French and Indian War. He was not a brilliant strategist, but he was very determined and faithful. He was able to win and hold the loyalty of the men who served under him. His religious beliefs were private, but appeared to follow traditional Christianity, not Deism. He believed deeply in the patriot cause and took a fearful chance when he agreed to lead the army. He would have been hanged as a traitor if the Americans had lost.

Washington did accept the commission from the Congress to lead the new "army." He refused to accept any pay, however, and asked only to be reimbursed for his expenses. He left at once for Boston and took command two weeks after Bunker Hill on July 2, 1775.

Choose the correct match for each item.

1.42 _____ Ethan Allen

1.43 _____ Shot Heard Around the World

1.44 _____ Artemas Ward

1.45 _____ valuable cannons captured

1.46 _____ fortified Breeds Hill

1.47 _____ militia fires along the road at British in retreat

1.48 _____ British destroy supplies, but are forced to retreat

1.49 _____ protects water route from Canada to New York

1.50 _____ Americans forced to quit when they run out of gunpowder

a. Lexington and Concord
b. Ticonderoga
c. Bunker Hill

1.51 _____ About half of the British forces are killed or wounded

1.52 _____ April 1775

1.53 _____ May 1775

1.54 _____ June 1775

Complete these sentences.

1.55 The assembled militia around Boston were taken as an American army by the _____ .

1.56 After the occupation of Boston, the American _____ began to drill and gather supplies.

1.57 Congress appointed _____ as commander-in-chief of the colonial army.

Olive Branch Petition. Congress was still hoping that the British government would come to terms and they could end this revolt. The Americans blamed most of what had happened on Parliament. They still declared their loyalty to the king. In July of 1775, the Congress made one last attempt to stop the war. At the insistence of John Dickinson of Delaware, the colonists prepared a petition directed to the king in July of 1775. The "Olive Branch Petition" affirmed their loyalty to the crown and asked the king to intervene with Parliament on behalf of the colonists. The petition was sent to Britain in the hands of one of William Penn's descendants. The king refused to even receive him. Instead he declared the colonies to be in rebellion.

The king further alienated the colonists by hiring German soldiers to fight the Americans. This was a common practice among European powers. Germany was divided into many small states, each with their own army. The kings would hire out these well-disciplined men to raise money. The Americans were shocked by the involvement of the foreign "Hessians" (many of the mercenaries came from the German state of Hesse) and many who had favored the king now joined the patriots.

Invasion of Canada. The war continued even while Congress and the country debated what to do. Several of the colonial leaders thought that the French Canadians might be persuaded to join the rebellion. In any case, New England needed to be secure from invasion from the North. So, American Generals Richard Montgomery and Benedict Arnold led an assault on Canada in late 1775.

Montgomery led his forces up from Lake Champlain and successfully captured Montreal. He then met up with Arnold at Quebec. Arnold's men had been struck by disease and reduced to eating shoe leather on their long march through the wilds of Maine. Still, the commanders attempted an attack in December. It failed miserably. Montgomery was killed. Arnold was wounded in the leg and retreated after a siege failed. The French, who had been treated generously by the Quebec Act, did not join the Americans; they remained firmly on the British side.

Common sense. The double life most Americans were leading, fighting British soldiers while declaring loyalty to the British crown, was shattered in early 1776 by the publication of a pamphlet called *Common Sense*. *Common Sense* was written by Thomas Paine, a recently arrived English immigrant. It was one of the most influential pamphlets ever written. Paine argued that British control over America was a violation of common sense. Why should an island rule over a continent? The colonists had no reason to be loyal to a king who had treated them so harshly. The Americans had a clear choice between independence or tyranny.

Common Sense was a phenomenal best seller. The pamphlet sold hundreds of thousands of copies in a few months. Public opinion turned in favor of independence. The American people decided to cross the line from loyal subjects defending their rights to a free and independent nation. Delegates at the Second Continental Congress were instructed by their state governments to vote for independence.

Declaration of Independence. On June 7, 1776 Richard Henry Lee of Virginia proposed to the Second Continental Congress that "These United Colonies are, and of right ought to be, free and independent states..." Debate began on the proposal and, since it was expected to pass, a committee was appointed to write a document explaining their reasons. The committee included Thomas Jefferson, John Adams, and Benjamin Franklin. As the best writer in the group, Jefferson was elected to do the writing. The other members only made suggestions after they had seen his draft of the paper.

| The signing of the Declaration of Independence

Jefferson's document became one of the most famous in American history. It included a brilliant preamble which was accepted by Congress without any changes. The remainder, a list of the acts of tyranny committed by the king and the actual statement that the colonies were now independent, were accepted with some changes. The document was accepted by Congress on July 4, 1776. A perfect copy was written and signed later by fifty-six of the delegates, including the president of the congress, John Hancock, who deliberately signed in very large letters. That bold act was the origin of the American saying that a person's signature is their "John Hancock."

The Fourth of July is celebrated as Independence Day in the United States. Congress voted for independence, in favor of Lee's proposal, on July 2, 1776. The day the Declaration of Independence was accepted, July 4th, has become the holiday. That document is simply too vibrant and stirring to take a second place to anything. You will study why as you examine the document in the next few pages.

Match these items.

1.58 _____ American general killed; invasion of Canada
1.59 _____ Congressman who insisted on one more petition to the king in July of 1775
1.60 _____ author of *Common Sense*
1.61 _____ American general wounded in the invasion of Canada
1.62 _____ Congressman who proposed independence
1.63 _____ author of the Declaration of Independence
1.64 _____ president of the Second Continental Congress

a. Richard Henry Lee
b. Thomas Paine
c. Thomas Jefferson
d. Richard Montgomery
e. John Dickinson
f. Benedict Arnold
g. John Hancock

Complete these sentences.

1.65 The Second Continental Congress sent a petition called the _____ Petition to request the king's help in July of 1775.

1.66 Montgomery succeeded in capturing the Canadian city of _____ .

1.67 American public opinion was turned in favor of independence by the popular pamphlet called _____ .

1.68 Congress voted for independence on _____ .

1.69 The American Revolution was fought for _____ months before independence was declared.

The American Revolution (1763–1789) | Unit 3

The unanimous Declaration of the thirteen united States of America,

When in the Course of human events, it becomes necessary for one people to dissolve the political bands which have connected them with another, and to assume among the powers of the earth, the separate and equal station to which the Laws of Nature and of Nature's God entitle them, a decent respect to the opinions of mankind requires that they should declare the causes which impel them to the separation.

We hold these truths to be self-evident, that all men are created equal, that they are endowed by their Creator with certain unalienable Rights, that among these are Life, Liberty and the pursuit of Happiness.—That to secure these rights, Governments are instituted among Men, deriving their just powers from the consent of the governed, —That whenever any Form of Government becomes destructive of these ends, it is the Right of the People to alter or to abolish it, and to institute new Government, laying its foundation on such principles and organizing its powers in such form, as to them shall seem most likely to effect their Safety and Happiness. Prudence, indeed, will dictate that Governments long established should not be changed for light and transient causes; and accordingly all experience hath shewn, that mankind are more disposed to suffer, while evils are sufferable, than to right themselves by abolishing the forms to which they are accustomed. But when a long train of abuses and usurpations, pursuing invariably the same Object evinces a design to reduce them under absolute Despotism, it is their right, it is their duty, to throw off such Government, and to provide new Guards for their future security.—Such has been the patient sufferance of these Colonies; and such is now the necessity which constrains them to alter their former Systems of Government. The history of the present King of Great Britain is a history of repeated injuries and usurpations, all having in direct object the establishment of an absolute Tyranny over these States. To prove this, let Facts be submitted to a candid world.

He has refused his Assent to Laws, the most wholesome and necessary for the public good.

He has forbidden his Governors to pass Laws of immediate and pressing importance, unless suspended in their operation till his Assent should be obtained; and when so suspended, he has utterly neglected to attend to them.

He has refused to pass other Laws for the accommodation of large districts of people, unless those people would relinquish the right of Representation in the Legislature, a right inestimable to them and formidable to tyrants only.

He has called together legislative bodies at places unusual, uncomfortable, and distant from the depository of their public Records, for the sole purpose of fatiguing them into compliance with his measures.

THE DECLARATION OF INDEPENDENCE
IN CONGRESS, July 4, 1776.

He has dissolved Representative Houses repeatedly, for opposing with manly firmness his invasions on the rights of the people.

He has refused for a long time, after such dissolutions, to cause others to be elected; whereby the Legislative powers, incapable of Annihilation, have returned to the People at large for their exercise; the State remaining in the mean time exposed to all the dangers of invasion from without, and convulsions within.

He has endeavoured to prevent the population of these States; for that purpose obstructing the Laws for Naturalization of Foreigners; refusing to pass others to encourage their migrations hither, and raising the conditions of new Appropriations of Lands.

He has obstructed the Administration of Justice, by refusing his Assent to Laws for establishing Judiciary powers.

He has made Judges dependent on his Will alone, for the tenure of their offices, and the amount and payment of their salaries.

He has erected a multitude of New Offices, and sent hither swarms of Officers to harrass our people, and eat out their substance.

He has kept among us, in times of peace, Standing Armies without the Consent of our legislatures.

He has affected to render the Military independent of and superior to the Civil power.

He has combined with others to subject us to a jurisdiction foreign to our constitution, and unacknowledged by our laws; giving his Assent to their Acts of pretended Legislation:

For Quartering large bodies of armed troops among us:

For protecting them, by a mock Trial, from punishment for any Murders which they should commit on the Inhabitants of these States:

For cutting off our Trade with all parts of the world:

For imposing Taxes on us without our Consent:

For depriving us in many cases, of the benefits of Trial by Jury:

For transporting us beyond Seas to be tried for pretended offences:

For abolishing the free System of English Laws in a neighbouring Province, establishing therein an Arbitrary government, and enlarging its Boundaries so as to render it at once an example and fit instrument for introducing the same absolute rule into these Colonies:

For taking away our Charters, abolishing our most valuable Laws, and altering fundamentally the Forms of our Governments:

For suspending our own Legislatures, and declaring themselves invested with power to legislate for us in all cases whatsoever.

The Declaration of Independence
IN CONGRESS, July 4, 1776.

He has abdicated Government here, by declaring us out of his Protection and waging War against us.

He has plundered our seas, ravaged our Coasts, burnt our towns, and destroyed the lives of our people.

He is at this time transporting large Armies of foreign Mercenaries to compleat the works of death, desolation and tyranny, already begun with circumstances of Cruelty & perfidy scarcely paralleled in the most barbarous ages, and totally unworthy the Head of a civilized nation.

He has constrained our fellow Citizens taken Captive on the high Seas to bear Arms against their Country, to become the executioners of their friends and Brethren, or to fall themselves by their Hands.

He has excited domestic insurrections amongst us, and has endeavoured to bring on the inhabitants of our frontiers, the merciless Indian Savages, whose known rule of warfare, is an undistinguished destruction of all ages, sexes and conditions.

In every stage of these Oppressions We have Petitioned for Redress in the most humble terms: Our repeated Petitions have been answered only by repeated injury. A Prince whose character is thus marked by every act which may define a Tyrant, is unfit to be the ruler of a free people.

Nor have We been wanting in attentions to our British brethren. We have warned them from time to time of attempts by their legislature to extend an unwarrantable jurisdiction over us. We have reminded them of the circumstances of our emigration and settlement here. We have appealed to their native justice and magnanimity, and we have conjured them by the ties of our common kindred to disavow these usurpations, which, would inevitably interrupt our connections and correspondence. They too have been deaf to the voice of justice and of consanguinity. We must, therefore, acquiesce in the necessity, which denounces our Separation, and hold them, as we hold the rest of mankind, Enemies in War, in Peace Friends.

We, therefore, the Representatives of the United States of America, in General Congress, Assembled, appealing to the Supreme Judge of the world for the rectitude of our intentions, do, in the Name, and by Authority of the good People of these Colonies, solemnly publish and declare, That these United Colonies are, and of Right ought to be Free and Independent States; that they are Absolved from all Allegiance to the British Crown, and that all political connection between them and the State of Great Britain, is and ought to be totally dissolved; and that as Free and Independent States, they have full Power to levy War, conclude Peace, contract Alliances, establish Commerce, and to do all other Acts and Things which Independent States may of right do. And for the support of this Declaration, with a firm reliance on the protection of divine Providence, we mutually pledge to each other our Lives, our Fortunes and our sacred Honor.

THE DECLARATION OF INDEPENDENCE
IN CONGRESS, July 4, 1776.

Unit 3 | **The American Revolution (1763–1789)**

Answer these questions.

1.70 Which full paragraph(s) are the preamble? _____

1.71 The center section lists the grievances against the crown and Parliament as well as the American attempts to gain a fair hearing. What are the phrases that begin and end this section?

   a. Beginning phrase: _____

   b. Ending phrase: _____

1.72 Which paragraph(s) are the statement of independence? _____

Do this activity.

1.73 In a class setting, read the preamble aloud and discuss what each phrase means. In an independent study setting, read the preamble (aloud, if possible) and write out what it means in your own words.

TEACHER CHECK _____ _____
                  initials   date

Look at the list of grievances in the Declaration. For each incident listed below give the phrase in the Declaration that refers to it (enough to identify it).

1.74 The dissolution of the colonial assemblies

_____
_____

1.75 The use of royal authority to veto colonial laws

_____
_____

1.76 The use of income from the Townshend Acts to pay salaries of officials

_____
_____

1.77 The Stamp Act

_____
_____

The American Revolution (1763–1789) | Unit 3

1.78 Use of Admiralty Courts
_____
_____

1.79 Changing the Massachusetts charter
_____
_____

1.80 Closing Boston Harbor
_____
_____

1.81 Encouraging Native American attacks
_____
_____

1.82 Hiring of Hessians
_____
_____

1.83 Quartering Act
_____
_____

1.84 Setting up a military government in Boston
_____
_____

1.85 Quebec Act
_____
_____

Review the material in this section in preparation for the Self Test. The Self Test will check your mastery of this particular section. The items missed on this Self Test will indicate specific areas where restudy is needed for mastery.

SELF TEST 1

Match the following people (each answer, 2 points).

1.01 _____ Boston radical; started Committees of Correspondence

1.02 _____ American commander at Ticonderoga and the invasion of Canada

1.03 _____ commander-in-chief of American army

1.04 _____ Prime Minister of Britain; Stamp Act

1.05 _____ author of the Declaration of Independence

1.06 _____ *Letters from a Farmer in Pennsylvania*; Olive Branch Petition

1.07 _____ Chancellor of the Exchequer; Britain

1.08 _____ Prime Minister who gave East India Company a monopoly on American tea sales

1.09 _____ president of Second Continental Congress; large signer of Declaration of Independence

1.010 _____ colonial representative in London before the war

a. George Grenville
b. Benjamin Franklin
c. Charles Townshend
d. John Dickinson
e. Lord North
f. Samuel Adams
g. John Hancock
h. George Washington
i. Benedict Arnold
j. Thomas Jefferson

Describe each of these giving the important points.

1.011 Stamp Act (5 points)

_____

_____

1.012 Townshend Acts (5 points)

_____

_____

1.013 Boston Massacre (5 points)

_____

_____

The American Revolution (1763–1789) | Unit 3

1.014 Boston Tea Party (4 points)

_____
_____

1.015 The Intolerable Acts (5 points)

_____
_____
_____

1.016 Quebec Act (5 points)

_____
_____
_____

1.017 Battle of Bunker Hill (5 points)

_____
_____
_____
_____

1.018 Colonial reaction to the Stamp Act (6 points)

a. _____   b. _____

c. _____

Complete these sentences (each answer, 3 points).

1.019 British policy toward the Thirteen Colonies was based on the economic theory of _____ .

1.020 The laws that were passed in the late 1600s, but rarely enforced, that restricted America to trade to the benefit of England were called the _____ Acts.

1.021 The _____ Act was passed when the Stamp Act was repealed and stated that Parliament could tax the colonies.

1.022 The _____ were secret societies opposed to British power that led mob action.

1.023 The _____ Act required colonists to house and feed British troops.

1.024 The _____ Act kept high taxes on sugar and rum and allowed violators to be tried in Admiralty Court.

1.025 The First Continental Congress met in response to the _____ Acts.

1.026 The Revolutionary War began at _____ .

1.027 The key fort, with its cannon, that was captured on Lake Champlain was Fort _____ .

1.028 _____ was an influential pamphlet written by Thomas Paine that urged America to become independent.

The American Revolution (1763–1789) | Unit 3

Answer true or false (each answer, 1 point).

1.029 _____ Britain was deeply in debt after the Seven Years War.

1.030 _____ The colonists carefully obeyed the trade laws before 1763.

1.031 _____ The American invasion of Canada encouraged the French colonists to rebel against the British.

1.032 _____ Congress voted for independence on July 4, 1776.

1.033 _____ The king's decision to use German mercenaries to fight in America turned many Americans against the British.

1.034 _____ The Olive Branch Petition was an offer of surrender by the American army after the defeat at Bunker Hill.

1.035 _____ The American army was organized from militia units.

1.036 _____ In 1773 Boston was the only city that refused to accept for sale the tea shipped in under the new monopoly to the East India Company.

1.037 _____ Britain wanted the Americans to bear some of the cost of their own defense.

1.038 _____ The colonies were always short of hard money because of British laws.

2. WAR

The Revolutionary War was fought from 1775 until 1783. Most of it was very discouraging for the Americans. They rarely won battles. They were always short of gunpowder, uniforms, boots, food, and cannons. Most of the soldiers in the army were militia. They only stayed for short periods of time. Some would return home each spring for planting or to deal with Native Americans in their state. The army was in a constant state of change, growing smaller and larger as men came and went. But, this very unlikely group held off the well-trained, well-supplied, well-disciplined British army for years.

Washington was forced by his circumstances to fight a defensive war. He wanted to attack and drive the British out of America, but he never had an army that could do that. Instead, he fought and retreated, forcing the British to keep their army ready to face him, but never giving them a decisive victory. The British captured cities but could not capture the hearts of the people. Eventually, the vengeful nations of Europe stepped in to reduce British power by helping the Americans. In the end, the war went to the Americans who won by simply surviving and not giving up.

SECTION OBJECTIVES

Review these objectives. When you have completed this section, you should be able to:

1. Identify the men who contributed to the Revolution.
3. Identify and describe the governing bodies that acted for the colonies/states.
4. Name the major battles of the war and to tell their significances.
5. Outline the terms of the peace agreements that the United States signed with Britain.

VOCABULARY

Study these words to enhance your learning success in this section.

asset (as' et). An advantage.

enlistment (en list' ment). The time for which a person joins some part of the armed forces.

guerrillas (gu ril' u). Fighters who harass the enemy by sudden raids; ambushes; the plundering of supplies and the like.

mediocre (mē' dē ō' ker). Of average quality; ordinary.

morale (mu ral'). Mental condition in regard to courage, confidence, or enthusiasm.

America Alone

British situation. The British appeared to have huge advantages over their American opponents in this war. They had a professional army of thousands, trained and ready to go. They also had the means to hire Hessians to add to their strength (eventually 30,000 served under the British in America). The British navy controlled the Atlantic. This was a tremendous advantage. The army could be moved, supplied, and reinforced anywhere along the coast, where most of the American population and all of the American cities were located.

Also, the British could count on the support of Americans still loyal to the crown. About one-third of the colonists were Loyalists or Tories. These were formidable **assets**.

However, the British also had several weaknesses. They had to fight this war across an ocean 3,000 miles (4,839 km) away. New information and orders could take months to reach a commander in the field from London. Britain also had no great leaders in power to organize the fight and most of her generals were **mediocre**. The other countries of Europe were anxious to take down British power, and might be willing to support the Americans. Moreover, the British had to defeat and conquer a huge area of territory and an uncooperative population. An incomplete victory would be no victory.

American situation. The Americans had the advantage of fighting near their homes for a righteous cause. They had outstanding leadership in men like George Washington, Nathanael Greene, Benedict Arnold, and Daniel Morgan. They were a tough, capable people who had already proven their courage and strength by leaving the safety of Europe to tame a wilderness land. The Americans learned to shoot while hunting for food. They were usually better shots than the British soldiers. Moreover, the Americans had the wide spaces of the country in which to retreat and hide.

The Americans also had deep weaknesses. Only about one third of the people supported the Revolution. America did not have an effective central government. The Second Continental Congress became the first government because there was no other body that could do it. It had no official authority. A system of government for the colonies, the Articles of Confederation, was not set up until 1781. The Congress had no power to tax and the money it printed lost value until it was practically worthless. The different states fought with each other constantly and usually put the needs of their state above the needs of the "nation."

Boston. General Washington was camped with the American army around Boston in early 1776. He had been there since July and the army had been there since Lexington in April. Washington's main accomplishment through that time was that he managed to keep the army there at all. Most of the militia were there only for short periods of **enlistment**, some as short as eight months. Gradually, Washington convinced some of them to stay and others to join. But, he did not have the strength to threaten the British in Boston, at least, not until Henry Knox arrived from Ticonderoga in March of 1776 with the fort's cannons.

The cannons changed the entire situation. Washington had them installed on Dorchester Heights, a high hill directly across from Boston. From there Washington could fire at will on the British in the city. The new British commander, Sir William Howe, gathered his men to attack, but a storm prevented them from crossing the bay. Instead, the British abandoned Boston, withdrawing to Canada.

Charleston. The British hoped to gain the support of Loyalists in the South by a show of force there. A force was organized for an assault in the spring of 1776. A Loyalist force of about 1,500 that intended to join up with the British was destroyed by Patriot forces in February. The defeat disheartened the Loyalists who made no attempt to join with the British when they finally arrived. Orders from London calling off the assault because of the Loyalists' defeat reached the commander, Henry Clinton, too late.

The British assault force, including ten warships and thirty transports, reached Charleston in June, 1776. The city, however, was well prepared. Sturdy forts had been built on the approaches to the harbor, and they were well supplied. The defenders were organized and calm. The British assault failed, driven back by the steady fire from the forts. The South was left in peace for the time being.

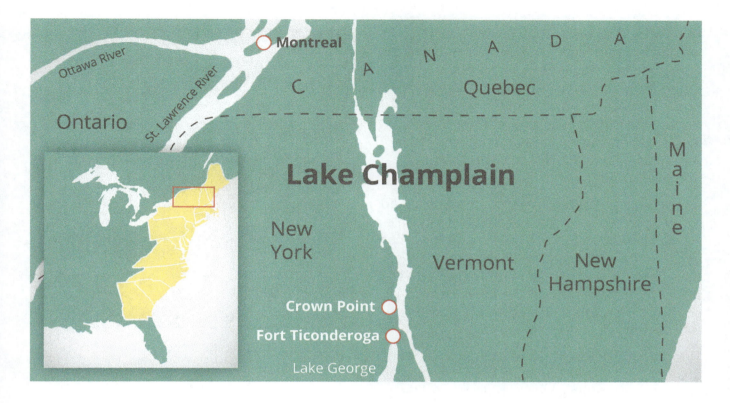

Lake Champlain. When Benedict Arnold retreated from Quebec in May of 1776, he headed back down Lake Champlain. The British governor in Canada, Sir Guy Carleton, followed. Carleton assembled a fleet to take troops down the lake. Arnold, now a brigadier general, constructed a ramshackle fleet to oppose them. The two sides met in October of 1776 on Lake Champlain. The American fleet was destroyed, but it succeeded in inflicting enough damage that Carleton withdrew for the season. Arnold's success at keeping the British from taking Fort Ticonderoga in 1776 was a key victory. It meant that the British invasion from Canada in 1777 had to start in Canada, not New York! Those would be precious miles and months for the Americans.

New York. The British withdrawal from Boston left Washington in a difficult position. The British had control of the seas and could attack anywhere they wanted along the coast. Washington would then have to march his men overland to meet them. Fortunately, Washington expected them to go to New York City, and they did. The army was shifted there to meet them.

The British arrived in July of 1776 with a huge force including more than 30,000 soldiers and 30 battleships. They took Staten Island to use as a base. The American position was impossible from the start. New York City is built on an island and the British controlled the waterways. They could land at will and prevent Washington from moving across the rivers. Washington had to defend everywhere at once. The British expected Washington to simply submit to British rule in the face of their control of the waterways and superior troop strength. They sent a few ships to fire on the city to prove their point. But, Washington refused to submit.

The British launched an assault on Long Island in August of 1776. The Americans had more than 10,000 men waiting for them. But, the British did not go straight up the hill into the fortifications as they did at Bunker Hill. Part of the British forces came around to attack from the rear. The inexperienced Americans panicked. By the end of the day, the survivors had retreated to Brooklyn Heights, near the ocean where the British navy prevented an escape.

But, Washington was not so easily trapped. He had his men leave their campfires burning and, under the cover of night, transferred the entire army across to Manhattan Island in small boats. The Americans retreated up the island leaving the British in control of New York City. The Battle of Long Island had been a serious American defeat, but the army had escaped and would fight again.

It was during this campaign that the British captured an American officer named Nathan Hale. He was behind the British lines trying to gather information. He was hung as a spy the next day without a trial. He said before he died, "I regret that I have but one life to lose for my country." He is remembered and honored for his bravery.

The British followed their success with more of the same. The Americans had built two forts, Washington and Lee, to secure New York City. Both held large supplies of American gunpowder, cannons, clothing, and war material. The British captured both forts and all of the 3,000 defenders.

| Nathan Hale's homestead

It was a staggering loss for the Americans. The British commander, William Howe, then settled down to enjoy the winter in the comfort of New York City since armies traditionally did not fight in the colder months.

These are the times that try men's souls. The summer soldier and the sunshine patriot will, in this crisis, shrink from the service of their country; but he that stands it now, deserves the love and thanks of man and woman. Tyranny, like hell, is not easily conquered; yet we have this consolation with us, that the harder the conflict, the more glorious the triumph. What we obtain too cheap, we esteem too lightly: it is dearness only that gives every thing its value.

Heaven knows how to put a proper price upon its goods; and it would be strange indeed if so celestial an article as FREEDOM should not be highly rated. Britain, with an army to enforce her tyranny, has declared that she has a right (not only to TAX) but "to BIND us in ALL CASES WHATSOEVER," and if being bound in that manner, is not slavery, then is there not such a thing as slavery upon earth. Even the expression is impious; for so unlimited a power can belong only to God.

THE AMERICAN CRISIS
Thomas Paine

Washington's men withdrew into New Jersey. They were in bad shape. They had been retreating for months. They lacked food and proper clothing. Thomas Paine, author of *Common Sense*, was with the army during this bleak hour. On a drumhead he wrote an essay that even today stirs the hearts of those who must face unexpected hardship in fighting for what they believe.

In each case, check the side that had the advantage.

		British	Americans
2.1	size of army	☐	☐
2.2	professionalism	☐	☐
2.3	commanders	☐	☐
2.4	government	☐	☐
2.5	location of the war	☐	☐
2.6	hope of foreign alliances	☐	☐
2.7	money and supplies	☐	☐
2.8	control of the sea	☐	☐
2.9	shooting accuracy	☐	☐
2.10	national unity	☐	☐

Answer these questions.

2.11 What was Washington's main accomplishment from July 1775 until March 1776?
_____

2.12 What gave the Americans the advantage in Boston?
_____

2.13 Why was Arnold's defeat on Lake Champlain in 1776 so important to the Americans?
_____

2.14 What was the result of the 1776 assault on Charleston?
_____

2.15 What happened to the Americans at the Battle of Long Island?
_____
_____

2.16 Who was Nathan Hale and what happened to him?

_____

_____

2.17 What happened to Forts Washington and Lee?

_____

2.18 How did the Continental Army escape after the Battle of Long Island?

_____

2.19 What was the condition of Washington's army going into winter 1776?

_____

According to Thomas Paine.

2.20 Why is tyranny like hell? _____ .

2.21 Unlimited power belongs only to _____ .

2.22 Those that shrink from the service of their country are _____

_____ .

2.23 If we obtain something too easily we will _____ .

Trenton. By the end of 1776, Washington was in a fix. He had experienced nothing but defeat since the evacuation of Boston. **Morale** was low. Many people were calling for him to be replaced. The enlistments of most of his men would run out at the end of the year. By January, the Americans might not even have any army. The Americans, now in Pennsylvania, desperately needed a victory. So, Washington took a huge gamble and prepared to attack.

On Christmas night 1776, Washington and his army made a dangerous trip across the ice-choked Delaware River. Early the next morning, the Americans attacked the Hessian army at Trenton, New Jersey. Surprise was complete. Most of the Germans were still in bed, sleeping off the celebrations of the day before. It was all over in less than an hour. Washington's army captured over a thousand men and their supplies. The victory convinced many of the men to stay in the army for at least a little longer.

Princeton. British General Charles Cornwallis rushed to Trenton in an attempt to trap Washington's army in January of 1777. The larger, better supplied British force caught the Americans at Trenton with their backs to the river. But, again, the cagey Washington refused to be trapped. He left his fires burning and a few volunteers who made noise in the camp while the rest of the army snuck away after dark. The Americans swung around the British force and attacked their reinforcements at Princeton, winning yet another battle. From there Washington retreated to easily defended highlands near Morristown, Pennsylvania for the rest of the winter.

The twin victories at Trenton and Princeton saved the American cause. Volunteers came in from all over the colonies. Many of the experienced troops agreed to stay, some of them serving until the end of the war. Washington's command was secure and never was seriously questioned again. But, these were only small victories.

Washington, summer of 1777. Sir William Howe was in command of the British forces in New York. The British strategy for that year called for him to move his men up the Hudson River to meet General Burgoyne who was invading from Canada. Howe's orders, however, were not clear, and he had already committed his soldiers to a campaign against Washington in the central states.

Howe tried, at first, to draw Washington into a battle around New York. When that failed, he decided to take his army by sea up the Chesapeake to attack Philadelphia in July. He believed he had plenty of time to help Burgoyne should the need arise.

Howe fought two battles with Washington en route to Philadelphia. The Americans lost both at Brandywine Creek (September) and Germantown (October). But, again the American army was not captured.

The loss at Germantown, moreover, impressed foreign observers. The Americans had initiated the attack and had been driven off only after heavy fighting. Also, the men had fought well against the experienced British army. But, they could not keep Howe from capturing Philadelphia.

The capture of the capital should have been a major victory for the British. But, it accomplished very little. Congress simply moved elsewhere. There were very few government officials or offices to move. Howe again settled down to spend a comfortable winter in yet another American city. But, Washington's army was still in the field and America was not yet conquered.

| Washington and his men crossing the Delaware

Valley Forge. The Continental army faced many hardships in the long years of the Revolution. Perhaps the most famous was their stay at Valley Forge, outside of Philadelphia in the winter of 1777-78. The very name of the place has become synonymous with suffering.

Washington had to stay near Philadelphia in case Howe decided to attack, and Valley Forge was one of his few choices for winter quarters. The army came in having lost two major battles, and the nation's capital. Thanks to a lack of funds, hoarding, corruption, and poor transport the troops were constantly short of supplies. In December, Washington wrote to Congress that 2,873 of his men were unfit for duty because they were barefoot or otherwise in need of clothes. Men left bloody tracks in the snow from their unprotected feet. Food was scarce and disease common.

The army's main occupation that winter was survival. What was astonishing was that the army continued to exist. The dedicated men did not desert. In fact, the army managed to build its skills during this dark time. The Americans were good fighters as individuals, but they lacked training on how to work as a group. A German officer, Baron von Steuben, who spoke no English, drilled the men all through the long winter on how to maneuver and attack as a unit. In spite of the conditions, he managed to vastly improve the discipline and professionalism of the army. The hard work in Valley Forge would yield good fruit for the army in the future.

 Choose the correct match for each item.

2.24 _____ January 1777
2.25 _____ October 1777
2.26 _____ Winter 1777-78
2.27 _____ drilling by von Stueben
2.28 _____ capture of 1,000 Hessians
2.29 _____ Americans snuck behind Cornwallis to attack his reinforcements
2.30 _____ December 1776
2.31 _____ captured by Howe
2.32 _____ Washington's winter quarters
2.33 _____ Howe's winter quarters
2.34 _____ Americans crossed the icy Delaware
2.35 _____ September 1777
2.36 _____ time of great suffering
2.37 _____ surprise attack, day after Christmas
2.38 _____ should have been major victory for British, did not accomplish much
2.39 _____ American army impressed foreign observers

a. Trenton
b. Princeton
c. Germantown
d. Brandywine Creek
e. Valley Forge
f. Philadelphia

The Turning Point

British plan. During the summer of 1777, the British had organized a master plan to cut New England off from the rest of the United States. The plan called for General Burgoyne to come down Lake Champlain and the Hudson River to Albany. Lieutenant Colonel St. Leger was to reach the same point by coming across from Lake Ontario and up the Mohawk River. In the meantime, General Howe was to come up the Hudson from New York and also reach Albany. This three-prong attack would conquer New York and isolate New England. The plan, however, required cooperation and the success of all three parts. As noted in the last section, General Howe received unclear orders from London and had already committed his troops to action in Pennsylvania. He never even made an attempt to join Burgoyne at Albany. The British master plan had all the makings of a grand disaster without the full support of all three commanders.

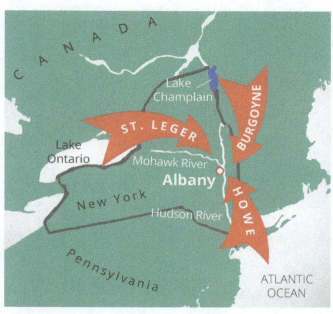

The unsuccessful British attack plan in the summer of 1777

St. Leger and the Battle of Oriskany.
Lt. Colonel Barry St. Leger was to bring a British force up the Mohawk Valley for his part in the campaign. He had a mixed force of about one thousand British, German, and Loyalist soldiers. He also had about the same number of Iroquois allies. The Americans in the valley knew what would happen if the Iroquois and the Loyalists, who were supporters of several autocratic landlords from the region, were to reach the rich farms of the region. They were prepared and ready to fight, ferociously.

St. Leger reached the American Fort Stanwix at what is now Rome, New York in late summer of 1777. The fort refused to surrender and skillfully held off his siege. The militia of the nearby towns sent a force of 800 under the command of General Nicholas Herkimer to aid the fort.

St. Leger heard of the relief effort and sent 1,200 soldiers and Iroquois to meet them. The British force set up an ambush near Oriskany Creek. The Americans walked into the trap on August 6th. They were driven to retreat, but not before they inflicted heavy losses on the British. In the meantime, Fort Stanwix's defenders had taken advantage of the situation to raid the British camp and carry off many of their supplies.

By now the Continental Army had been alerted and a force of 1,000 men under General Benedict Arnold was on route to Stanwix. St. Leger's men heard rumors of the force, and received exaggerated reports of its size. The Iroquois and Loyalists began to panic. In late August, St. Leger began a retreat to his base on Lake Ontario. General Burgoyne was now the only one of the three commanders still pursuing the planned advance on Albany.

The American Revolution (1763–1789) | Unit 3

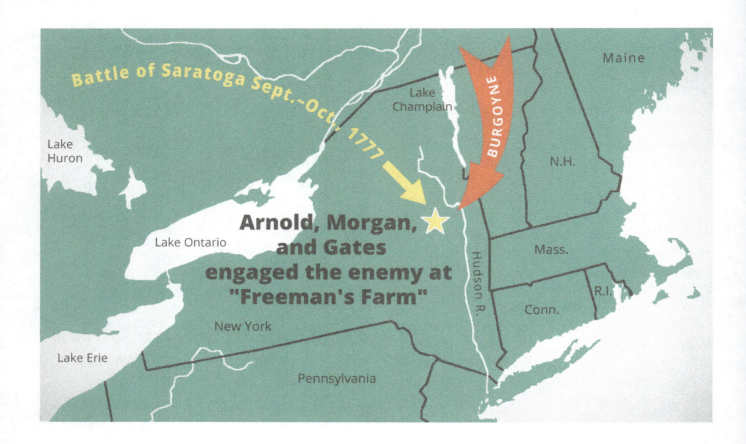

Burgoyne. John "Gentleman Johnny" Burgoyne was a popular and arrogant British general. He believed he would have no trouble with the American militia. He started down the Richelieu River to Lake Champlain in June of 1777. He had about 7,000 British and German troops under his command. He was also accompanied by a large contingent of about 400 Iroquois People. Burgoyne was handicapped by a huge baggage train, hundreds of camp followers, including women and children, and over a hundred cannons he insisted be brought along, some of them to be dragged with the army through the wilderness.

The force floated down Lake Champlain and reached Fort Ticonderoga in early July. The fort was held by Major General Arthur St. Clair and 2,000 men. An alert British engineer noticed the high hill called Mount Defiance that towered above the fort. The steep sides made it difficult to climb and no one among the Americans dreamed the British could haul cannons up there. But, they did. St. Clair realized his danger and evacuated the fort before he and his men could be trapped.

Burgoyne then proceeded to show his ignorance of wilderness warfare. He set off to cross the 23 miles between Lake Champlain and the Hudson River Valley building a road as he went. He also dragged his own thirty carts of personal belongings as well as dozens of cannons. By now the alarm had gone out all over New England and Americans were swarming around Burgoyne like flies. They made him pay for every step he took through those miles of wilderness. Trees were felled across his path. Rivers were dammed and low areas flooded. It took Burgoyne an entire month to reach the Hudson. Then, he had to wait for his supplies to reach him.

The Americans feared not only the British but the Iroquois they had with him. They had good reason to believe that Burgoyne could not control them. In fact, on the trip south, some of the Iroquois captured and scalped a young woman named Jane McCrea, the fiancée of one of the Loyalist officers. Burgoyne did not punish the murderer because the other Native Americans would have left if he did. The Americans made good use of the story to convince New Englanders that Burgoyne did not even protect those who were loyal to the crown. What would happen to Patriots that happened to fall into his hands? More and more citizens took up their guns and went to join the growing horde opposing the British advance.

Burgoyne sent out a small force in mid-August to secure some horses that were rumored to be at Bennington. The entire German unit was destroyed by the Americans. The British unit sent to help was driven back. Burgoyne refused to take warning from the defeat or the news that neither Howe nor St. Leger were coming.

Saratoga. Burgoyne pressed on down the Hudson Valley toward Albany in September. He took only the minimum of supplies his army would need for the short trip to Albany, but kept his own baggage and the cannons. Snipers made it dangerous to leave the camp. The Americans again burned bridges, flooded lowlands, and felled trees to slow him down. Burgoyne often made only a mile a day or less and it was getting near winter.

General Horatio Gates was sent by Congress to command the American forces. Daniel Morgan, with his sharp-shooting riflemen, and Benedict Arnold were also sent. (Rifles, which were just coming into use, were more accurate than the muskets used by the British, but they took longer to reload.) Washington was too busy with Howe in Pennsylvania to come or send many men. Most of the soldiers in the army that faced Burgoyne were simply citizens who came to defend their homeland.

The two armies met twice on a piece of land called Freeman's Farm in September and October. The Americans fought from behind trees and let the British have the open field. Morgan and Arnold, not Gates, were responsible for the victories. Morgan's riflemen defied every rule of polite warfare by shooting from up in the trees deliberately aiming for the officers! General Benedict Arnold displayed his brilliance as a field commander by leading a furious attack in the second battle. He was severely wounded in the same leg that was injured in the attack on Quebec. Most of the time the British could not even get a good look, much less a clear shot, at their enemies. The British were routed in both battles.

His army in shambles, Burgoyne retreated, hoping to reach the safety of Ticonderoga. The men had no warm clothes and the weather was getting colder. British supplies of food were also low and the Americans continued to harass them. Burgoyne dug in on some high ground near the village of Saratoga for a rest. The American army surrounded him. With no other alternative, Burgoyne surrendered his entire army of about 5,000 men on October 17, 1777.

Complete these sentences.

2.40 The British plan for 1777 called for _____ to lead an attack down Lake Champlain, _____ to come up the Mohawk Valley, and _____ to come up the Hudson from New York City.

2.41 St. Leger was unable to capture _____ in New York and his forces were badly hurt in the battle at _____ .

2.42 Burgoyne took Fort _____ on Lake Champlain by putting cannon on Mount _____ .

2.43 Burgoyne carried _____ cart loads of his own belongings, dozens of _____ and hundreds of camp followers with him.

2.44 The Americans made good use of propaganda in the murder of _____ _____ by the Iroquois.

2.45 An entire German unit was wiped out by the Americans at _____ .

2.46 The Americans defeated Burgoyne's forces in two battles at _____ .

2.47 The leaders of the American victory were _____ and _____ .

2.48 The official American commander was _____ .

2.49 Burgoyne surrendered his entire army at _____ in October 1777.

Significance of Saratoga. The victory at Saratoga was the turning point of the war. The Americans had defeated and captured an entire British army. The British evacuated Ticonderoga and withdrew to Canada. The victory brought great cheer to the American side. The victory also brought the Patriot cause much needed allies.

Franklin in France. The Americans knew how badly the French wanted revenge for their losses in the Seven Years War. It was natural, therefore, to seek assistance from them for the American Rebellion. Benjamin Franklin was sent to France as an official envoy in September, 1776 to get a possible alliance. The French were willing to encourage the colonists, but were not willing to immediately risk war with Britain. However, they did provide valuable weapons and supplies through a trading company called *Hortalez et Cie*, thus staying officially neutral.

Franklin quickly became one of the most popular men in France, the darling of the frivolous French court. The aristocracy was very interested in the theories of the day that taught the superiority of "natural man." Franklin agreeably played the part of the noble rustic, much to the delight of the high-born ladies. He did not wear the rich clothes, sword, and wig normally expected of a court envoy. Instead, he dressed plainly and acted the part of the natural philosopher, even occasionally wearing a fur cap. The French courtiers were enchanted, but the French leaders wanted proof that America could fight and win a war before they committed.

The victory at Saratoga along with the surprising American showing at Germantown provided the proof the French wanted. They signed a treaty of Alliance with the Americans in February of 1778, while Washington's men hungered in Valley Forge. The French navy could now be used to protect American trade and threaten the British West Indies. The Spanish and Dutch also eventually joined the alliance. Britain now had a world war, not a colonial rebellion on its hands.

| The Marquis de Lafayette

Lafayette. The Marquis de Lafayette was one of the many assets America received from France throughout the Revolution. Lafayette was a very wealthy French aristocrat who joined the American cause in 1777 at the age of nineteen. He was assigned as an aide to General Washington, and the two became very close friends. He was gradually given opportunities to command which he handled skillfully to the advantage of the American cause. He donated a great deal of money to the patriot cause and used his influence with the king of France to arrange for a French army to come to America in 1779. He has long been hailed as a hero of the Revolution and is honored in America by numerous towns that bear his name.

Monmouth. By early 1778, Sir Henry Clinton had replaced Howe as commander of the British forces in America. News of the alliance with France reached him in Philadelphia, which the British still held. He was ordered to evacuate Philadelphia and return to New York. Clinton decided to march his army north and Washington went to meet him. A battle was fought at Monmouth Court House in New Jersey. It would be the last major battle in the North.

Washington sent an advance strike force under the command of General Charles Lee, who had been a British prisoner for a time and had a poor attitude. Lee attacked as ordered, but then withdrew without any reason. Washington came up with the rest of the army to find the strike force in a disorderly retreat. It was one of the few times Washington publicly lost his temper. He charged into the retreating lines, ordered Lee to surrender his command, rallied the men, and led the fight himself (Lee was later court-martialed). The battle ended indecisively, and the British succeeded in reaching New York safely. The two sides were now back where they had been in 1776, the British bottled up in New York, the Americans watching and waiting. Washington would remain there until 1781.

Western campaign. Most of the battles in the west were fought against the Native American Peoples who were encouraged by the British to make raids on the American settlements. Control of this region would enable the patriots to concentrate on the east and south. In 1778 George Rogers Clark and a band of frontiersmen overcame the British at Kaskasia, Cahokia, and Vincennes, the three major British forts in the west. These victories brought the west under American control. Colonel Henry Hamilton, a British officer, however, recaptured Vincennes. His victory was short-lived as George Rogers Clark led his men 180 miles through waist-deep swamps in the dead of winter to recapture the fort and bring the west under American control. This would prove vital in the years after the Revolution because the area south of the Great Lakes was in American hands, not British. The Americans received little trouble from the Native Americans and British in the west for the remainder of the war.

The war at sea. The tiny American navy, made up mostly of privateers, was no match for the British navy, which was the largest in the world. Yet, under the leadership of John Paul Jones and John Barry, using European ports, the navy managed to harass British ships near England.

One of the most famous American-British sea battles took place in 1779 between the *Bonhomme Richard*, under the command of John Paul Jones, and the British warship *Serapis*. The two engaged in savage combat for over three hours. The *Bonhomme Richard* was badly damaged and sinking. Yet, Jones refused to surrender saying, "I have not yet begun to fight!" He eventually captured the *Serapis*. This and other victories did little for the American cause except in the area of morale. The only real chance the Americans had at sea came with the alliance that brought the French navy in on their side.

Treachery. One of the most disheartening events of the Revolution occurred in 1780 when Benedict Arnold became a traitor. The hero of Ticonderoga and Saratoga was bitter over some setbacks in his military career. He also had married a Loyalist and become fond of rich living. In September of 1780, he offered to turn over his command, the American fort at West Point that protected the upper Hudson River, to the British. In exchange, he was to receive a large amount of money and a commission in the British army.

The man acting as the go-between, Major John André, was captured with the plans of the fort in Arnold's handwriting. Arnold fled to New York before he could be captured and André was hanged as a spy. West Point was strengthened and never fell into British hands. But, the loss of such a trusted and successful commander was a blow to the Americans.

Arnold fought the remainder of the Revolution as a British Brigadier General, a step below his American rank of Major General. He lived the rest of his life as a British subject reviled by his former countrymen. His name became synonymous with traitor in the American language. But, his brilliant work for the American cause was not forgotten. At Saratoga there is a very unusual memorial. It is a statue of a leg, the leg of Benedict Arnold. Injured at both Quebec and Saratoga, it was the only loyal part of the former American hero.

Complete these sentences.

2.50 _____ was the turning point of the Revolutionary War.

2.51 France formed an alliance with the Americans after the battles of _____ and _____ .

2.52 _____ was a wealthy French aristocrat who became an American officer and hero.

2.53 America's representative in France was _____ who played the part of the "natural man" for the court.

2.54 The last major battle in the North was _____ and it was indecisive.

2.55 _____ took control of the British forts in the west with a small force of frontiersmen.

2.56 The Americans recaptured the fort at _____ from the British after marching 180 miles through waist deep water in the winter.

2.57 _____ betrayed his country by offering to turn over the fort at _____ to the British for money and an officer's commission.

2.58 _____ was court-martialed for retreating at Monmouth Courthouse.

2.59 _____ was the American naval commander who said, "I have not yet begun to fight," during the battle between the American ship _____ and the British ship _____ .

2.60 _____ was the spy captured by the Americans with the plans of West Point.

The End of the War

Georgia. The British plans had failed so miserably in the North that they decided to concentrate on the less populous South. Their plan was to capture each state, organize the Loyalists there to take control, and then move on to the next state. In 1779 a well-organized force captured Savannah and all of Georgia. An attempt to retake the city by a joint American-French force failed in October.

South Carolina. Sir Henry Clinton, in command in New York, now moved a force of about 10,000 south using the resources of the British navy. He successfully besieged Charleston avoiding the mistakes made in the earlier attempt. The city fell on May 12, 1780. The American commander, General Benjamin Lincoln, was captured along with 5,000 men, all of their supplies, and almost all of the Revolutionary leaders of South Carolina. It was the biggest single American disaster of the war.

Using Charleston as a base, Clinton sent out troops to secure the colony. In June, Clinton turned over command to Lord Cornwallis and returned to New York. Cornwallis set up a series of forts in the interior of South Carolina to protect the British gains. Soon all of South Carolina was under British control.

Camden. Congress sent a new army south to engage Cornwallis. They chose Horatio Gates, the official victor at Saratoga, to command the force. Gates lacked the skills needed for such a difficult job. The hastily assembled force was made up mainly of militia, which had never been in battle, and a few experienced units from the Continental Army. The two sides met at Camden, South Carolina in August 1780. It was a humiliating defeat for the Americans. Many of the inexperienced troops ran without firing a shot. The Continentals fought hard, but were overwhelmed when the rest of the army withdrew. Gates and the remains of his army fled north.

King's Mountain. The overconfident Cornwallis decided to attack North Carolina before South Carolina was fully secure. He sent an advance force of about a thousand Loyalists north under the command of Major Patrick Ferguson, a British officer. They ordered the North Carolina citizens to submit to the crown or face attack and occupation. The independent men of North Carolina not only refused, they gathered a force of backwoodsmen and went south to meet the British. They engaged the enemy at King's Mountain in South Carolina in October of 1780. It was one of the bloodiest battles of the war because the Patriots totally annihilated the Tory regiment.

Nathanael Greene. Congress now wisely asked Washington to recommend someone to take command of the shattered southern army. Washington chose Nathanael Greene. It was an ideal choice. Greene realized he did not have the strength to defeat Cornwallis in a pitched battle. So, he planned out and executed one of the most brilliant American campaigns of the war.

There were several bands of **guerrillas** active in the South. The most famous was under the command of Francis Marion, the "Swamp Fox." Greene made contact with these men and had his regular troops work with them. The guerrilla bands raided British outposts, harassed supply lines, and acted as scouts for the regular army. By coordinating with these bands, Greene managed to press the British and keep them off balance.

Greene used his regular army to draw Cornwallis into an extended chase all over Carolina. The British were drawn far from their supply bases and forced to take provisions from the local people. This made the British unpopular and strengthened the American cause in the South. Greene lost every major engagement he fought. But, he always inflicted severe losses on the British and escaped to fight again. "We fight, get beat, rise and fight again," was the way Greene described the campaign. By June of 1781, Greene and his guerrilla allies had made the Carolina countryside difficult for Cornwallis to handle. The British lost control of everything except the cities.

Cowpens. Greene had split his forces when he took command in 1780, in the hopes that Cornwallis would split his as well, giving the Americans a chance. Cornwallis cooperated sending a force of about a thousand after Daniel Morgan's eight hundred men. Morgan chose the place for the battle, a spot called the Cowpens. In January 1781, the British under Colonel Tarleton rode into the American trap. Faking a retreat, Morgan's men drew the British into a position to be attacked from all sides. Almost the entire force was killed or captured. It was the one major victory of the campaign.

A furious Cornwallis chased Morgan, who wisely withdrew. Then, Cornwallis took off in an exhausting chase to try and trap Greene. Greene's men managed to outrun him, and crossed the Dan River to safety in Virginia in February of 1781. Cornwallis was now far from his supply bases and constantly facing harassment from the Americans.

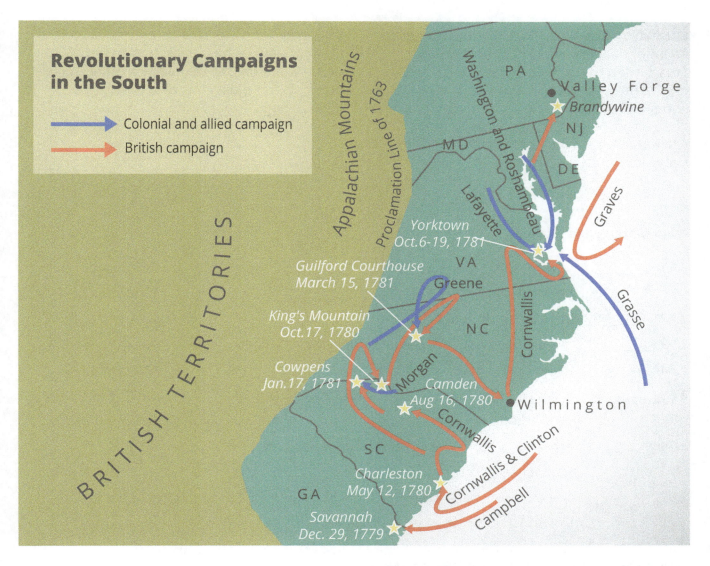

Guilford Courthouse. Greene came back into North Carolina after Cornwallis withdrew. He set his men up at a site he had selected in advance, Guilford Courthouse, North Carolina. Cornwallis chased him and arrived March 15th with a British force. The British technically won the battle because the Americans withdrew at the end of the day. But, Cornwallis lost one-fourth of his men, while the American casualties were light. Moreover, the American army was still intact. Cornwallis withdrew toward the sea to refit his force.

Falling forts. Greene then turned on the forts that held the Carolina interior. His forces were defeated at Hobkirk's Hill in April, but the British commander abandoned the nearby fort due to the heavy losses of men and supplies to the guerrilla forces. Other forts were captured by these forces while the army kept the British too busy to send aid. Greene's siege of another fort, Ninety-six, was broken by the British in May, but again the British decided the fort could not be held and withdrew. By June, almost the entire line of British forts were gone. Having lost most of the battles, Greene won the campaign. Most of the South was again in American hands.

The American Revolution (1763–1789) | Unit 3

Eutaw Springs. The British troops from the abandoned forts, under Colonel Alexander Stuart, tried to reach Cornwallis' army after resting through the hot summer. The Americans under Greene met them at Eutaw Springs near Charleston, South Carolina in September 1781. Again the Americans lost the battle, inflicting heavy losses on the British. Stuart withdrew to Charleston and did not attempt any further action for the remainder of the war. The British made no other major attempts to regain control in the South. It was a spectacular American victory.

Match these items.

2.61 _____ Loyalist force was destroyed by North Carolina backwoodsmen

2.62 _____ loss of Lincoln and 5,000 men

2.63 _____ humiliating American defeat under Horatio Gates

2.64 _____ taken by the British in 1779

2.65 _____ British troops under Stuart defeat Greene near Charleston

2.66 _____ American victory under Daniel Morgan against Colonel Tarleton's force

2.67 _____ Greene came back from North Carolina to draw Cornwallis into a battle where the British lost one fourth of their men

a. Savannah
b. Charleston
c. Camden
d. King's Mountain
e. Cowpens
f. Guilford Courthouse
g. Eutaw Springs

Name the person.

2.68 _____ the "Swamp Fox", Carolina guerrilla leader

2.69 _____ victorious commander at Cowpens

2.70 _____ American commander in the south who lost the battles and won the campaign

2.71 _____ victor at Saratoga, chosen by Congress to command American army in the South after the fall of Charleston

2.72 _____ British commander in the South after the withdrawal of Clinton

Yorktown. Lafayette had been sent south in 1781 with an American army to pursue Cornwallis, who was now busy in Virginia. Cornwallis was unable to pin down the cagey Frenchman. Meanwhile, Clinton decided he wanted some of Cornwallis' men to reinforce New York, for fear of an attack there. So, Cornwallis withdrew to Yorktown on Chesapeake Bay and set up a strong defensive position to wait for the British navy. But, it would be the French navy that came instead.

When Washington heard that Cornwallis was stationary on the sea coast, he grabbed a chance to capture a major British army. The Americans had the use of a French fleet under the command of Admiral de Grasse. Washington sent it to blockade the Chesapeake, cutting off Cornwallis' supply and escape route. The French navy successfully defeated the ships sent to relieve Cornwallis and blocked any hope of help from the sea.

While de Grasse moved into position, Washington and Rochambeau, the commander of the French army in America, moved south to trap Cornwallis. The American and French armies, numbering about 17,000, encircled the British camp which held about 10,000 men. Cornwallis was dug into a defensive position, but with the sea and the French navy behind him, he had no place to go.

The Allies set up siege lines under the direction of Rochambeau, who was an expert in this type of warfare. They began a steady pounding of the British lines with cannon fire. Slowly, the Americans and French moved closer and closer capturing the outer British defenses. With no hope of reinforcements or supplies, the result was inevitable. On October 17th, the British asked for surrender terms.

Cornwallis surrendered his entire command on October 19, 1781. The army marched out to the tune of "The World Turn'd Upside Down" and laid down their arms. Lord Cornwallis, claiming to be ill, sent General O'Hara to surrender for him. O'Hara first moved to surrender to the French, but was directed to Washington. Washington declined to receive Cornwallis' sword (the customary mark of a surrender) since the general did not choose to deliver it in person. Instead, Washington directed that it be surrendered to Benjamin Lincoln, the general who had suffered the greatest American defeat of the war, at Charleston.

Yorktown was the last major battle of the war, although neither side knew that. Both armies remained in the field for another two years, awaiting events in Europe that would finally bring a conclusion. In Britain the war had become immensely unpopular as British losses mounted both in America and in other areas. A new government came to power that was determined to make peace.

Treaty of Paris. Peace talks were opened in France in 1782 with the American delegation. The Americans included Benjamin Franklin, John Adams, and John Jay. A treaty was negotiated and signed on September 3, 1783 in Paris. The terms were very generous to the Americans because the British wanted to break up America's alliance with the French in the event of future wars.

The Treaty of Paris gave the Americans almost everything they wanted. America's independence was recognized, and all of the land east of the Mississippi between Canada and Florida was recognized as hers. All British forces were to leave American land. The Mississippi was open to American commerce and American ships could fish in the Newfoundland waters. Spain received Florida back, and the French got back the islands of the West Indies captured in the war. Congress was to recommend that Loyalists be given back their land and all debts owed to Britain were recognized as valid. The military phase of the Revolution was now over, but it was still not clear what kind of government would rule in America. That part of the Revolution was unfinished.

The American Revolution (1763–1789) | Unit 3

Washington's finest hour. The American economy was in a shambles at the end of the war. The money issued by Congress was worthless and the army had never been properly paid. In May of 1782, several of Washington's officers sent him a memo asking him to use the army and set himself up as a new king. This was the pattern of history when a victorious general has led a successful rebellion against a king. Washington coldly refused. When word of the peace treaty reached him in November of 1783, he defied the pattern of history and shocked most of the rulers of Europe by resigning his commission and retiring to private life. It was, in this author's opinion, the single greatest service Washington ever did for his country.

Answer these question.

2.73 How was Cornwallis trapped at Yorktown?
_____
_____

2.74 What was the name of the French army commander at Yorktown?
_____

2.75 What was the name of the French naval commander at Yorktown?
_____

2.76 Who negotiated the Treaty of Paris for America?
_____

2.77 Who received Cornwallis' sword at the surrender at Yorktown?
_____

2.78 Why was Washington's decision to resign his commission so important? (Think about it.)
_____
_____

2.79 What were the nine important terms of the Treaty of Paris?
1. _____
2. _____
3. _____
4. _____
5. _____
6. _____
7. _____
8. _____
9. _____

Unit 3 | **The American Revolution (1763–1789)**

SELF TEST 2

Match these people (each answer, 2 points).

2.01 _____ Lord Cornwallis
2.02 _____ Benedict Arnold
2.03 _____ Thomas Paine
2.04 _____ Burgoyne
2.05 _____ Benjamin Franklin
2.06 _____ Marquis de Lafayette
2.07 _____ Thomas Jefferson
2.08 _____ Samuel Adams
2.09 _____ George Rogers Clark
2.010 _____ John Paul Jones
2.011 _____ Benjamin Lincoln
2.012 _____ Nathanael Greene
2.013 _____ Daniel Morgan
2.014 _____ Rochambeau
2.015 _____ De Grasse

a. Boston radical; Committees of Correspondence
b. commanded greatest American defeat of the war; lost 5,000 men
c. British commander in the south, 1780-81
d. captured western British forts with small force of frontiersmen
e. French army commander
f. French admiral
g. author of *Common Sense* and *The American Crisis*
h. captain of the *Bonhomme Richard*
i. American commander in the South; lost all the battles but won the campaign
j. commanded riflemen at Freeman's Farm and the victorious Americans at Cowpens
k. French volunteer/hero in American army; close friend of Washington
l. British general; surrendered his entire army after campaign in Upstate New York
m. American hero turned traitor
n. American representative in France; played the "natural man" for the court
o. author of the Declaration of Independence

The American Revolution (1763–1789) | Unit 3

Choose the correct answer from the list (each answer, 3 points).

Saratoga   Long Island   Yorktown
Charleston   Camden   Oriskany
Monmouth Courthouse   Trenton   King's Mountain
Valley Forge

2.016 The last major battle in the North was an inconclusive conflict fought at _____ _____ between Washington's army and the army of Sir Henry Clinton who was moving back to New York.

2.017 Washington made a risky crossing of the icy Delaware River to attack the Hessians at _____ the day after Christmas 1776.

2.018 The surrender of the British army at _____ was the turning point of the war.

2.019 British commander St. Leger won the Battle of _____ when he ambushed an American force coming to the aid of Fort Stanwix.

2.020 A Tory army marching to attack North Carolina was met by a force of backwoodsmen from that state who annihilated them in 1780 at _____ .

2.021 The American army spent a cold, difficult winter at _____ improving their drilling skills under the teaching of Baron von Steuben.

2.022 The surrender of the British army at _____ , after it was trapped by the French navy and the combined French/American army, was the final major battle of the war.

2.023 The British defeated Washington at the Battle of _____ in 1776 by coming around and attacking from the rear of his inexperienced army and driving them back to Brooklyn Heights, where they skillfully slipped away after dark.

2.024 _____ was successfully defended in 1776, but was taken in 1780 in the biggest American disaster of the war.

2.025 Horatio Gates was humiliatingly defeated at _____ when he tried to lead an army south in 1780 to engage the victorious British after the conquest of Georgia and South Carolina.

Answer these questions (each answer, 3 points).

2.026 What nation signed a treaty of alliance with the Americans in 1778?
_____

2.027 Where did the cannons come from that drove the British out of Boston in 1776?
_____

2.028 In the summer of 1777, Washington fought the Battles of Brandywine Creek and Germantown trying to stop the British from reaching what city?
_____

2.029 The British colonies were ruled using what economic theory?
_____

2.030 What was the law that guaranteed the French in Canada their traditional laws and extended their land?
_____

2.031 What was the law that united the colonies against taxation without representation and was repealed after just four months of being in effect?
_____

2.032 The Intolerable Acts were the British reaction to what event?
_____

2.033 What were three advantages the British had in the Revolution?

a. _____

b. _____

c. _____

The American Revolution (1763–1789) | Unit 3

Answer true or false (each answer, 1 point).

2.034 _____ The Americans had the advantage of location in the war.

2.035 _____ Forts Washington and Lee near New York City were never taken by the British.

2.036 _____ The American army that fought at Freeman's Farm was mainly citizen soldiers who came to defend their homes.

2.037 _____ Nathan Hale said, "I have not yet begun to fight."

2.038 _____ Guilford Courthouse and Eutaw Springs were both British victories that hurt the victors more than the losers.

2.039 _____ The Navigation Acts were rarely enforced until after the Seven Years War.

2.040 _____ The Treaty of Paris gave the Americans very little of what they wanted.

2.041 _____ The Treaty of Paris granted America independence and promised they could use the Mississippi River.

2.042 _____ George Washington was not a great strategist, but he was faithful and had the loyalty of his men.

2.043 _____ Colonists tried in Admiralty Courts did not have a jury and were presumed to be guilty.

3. THE CONSTITUTION

A revolution is a tremendous change in events. The American Revolution changed the states of North America from separate colonies under a European monarchy, to a united nation under a Federal Republic. Thus, the Revolution is actually more than just the war. It also includes the process of establishing the new government in America.

It was not clear at the end of the Revolutionary War what sort of government the new nation would have. It was not even clear that it would be one nation. The people thought of themselves as citizens of their states, and might well have set up thirteen countries, with or without some sort of alliance between them.

The "government" that was set up during the war had very little authority and was not trusted by the people. The country was still unstable and could easily have slipped into a dictatorship of some kind.

The Revolution up until 1783 had been a revolt against the old system, now the Americans had to create a new one. This was not to be a war of guns, but a war of ideas. Victory was not to be won by conquest, but by compromise. The result of this part of the Revolution was the surprisingly successful Constitution of the United States of America.

SECTION OBJECTIVES

Review these objectives. When you have completed this section, you should be able to:

1. Identify the men who contributed to the Revolution.
3. Identify and describe the governing bodies that acted for the colonies/states.
6. Explain the Articles of Confederation and why they were replaced.
7. Describe the Constitutional Convention.
8. Describe the main features of the Constitution and the process by which it was approved.

VOCABULARY

Study these words to enhance your learning success in this section.

confederation (kun fed' u rā shun). A group of countries or states joined together for a special purpose; a league.

executive (eg zek' yu tiv). The person or branch of government that has the duty and power of putting laws into effect.

impeach (im pēch'). To accuse a public official of wrong conduct in office before a proper tribunal.

inflation (in flā' shun). A rise in the price of goods.

ratify (rat' u fī). To confirm or approve.

sovereign (sov' ren). Independent of the control of another government or governments.

The Articles of Confederation

The first constitution of the United States was called the Articles of **Confederation**. It was adopted by the Second Continental Congress in 1777. However, it could not go into effect until all thirteen of the states **ratified** it. That did not happen until 1781, and by 1789, it was superseded by the new Constitution. These eight years were a stepping stone between America's first government under the Second Continental Congress, and her permanent government under the Constitution.

America's first constitution. The Articles of Confederation formed only a "firm league of friendship" between the thirteen **sovereign** states of America. It was less than a union, but more than an alliance. The states kept the power to tax, regulate commerce, and provide justice. The central government was very weak, for good reason. The states would not have accepted gaining their freedom from Britain just to lose it to a more local tyrant! The Articles provided an in-between step that allowed them time to accept the need for a strong central government.

The national government under the Articles was very weak. The states did not want a strong **executive**, like the king, to threaten their liberties. So, the Articles had no executive to enforce the laws. There was also no national system of courts or judges. The Confederation was ruled by a very weak Congress.

Congress was deliberately limited in its power. It could not raise taxes, it could only request money from the states. It also could not regulate commerce between the states. The voting in the Congress was one representative per state. All important matters had to be passed by two-thirds of the states and any changes to the Articles had to be unanimous. Congress was supposed to conduct the Confederation's foreign affairs (including those with the Native Americans), declare war, establish an army and navy, set up a postal service, and settle disputes between the states.

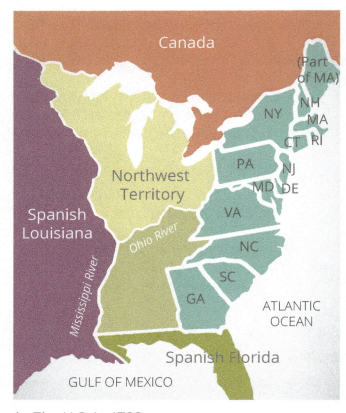

| The U.S. in 1783

But, without a steady source of income or authority to enforce its laws, Congress was severely shackled in its efforts to act for the nation.

The Northwest Territory. In spite of its weaknesses, the Congress under the Articles had one very notable success. That was the handling of the Northwest Territory. The Northwest Territory (or Old Northwest) was the land west of the established states and north of the Ohio River. This land came under the control of Congress shortly after the ratification of the Articles of Confederation.

Several of the original colonies had been granted in their charters rights to vast amounts of land west of the Appalachians. The states who did not have land claims there, notably Pennsylvania and Maryland, insisted that all of the western lands be given to the national government.

They argued the land-rich states could use land sales to pay off debts from the Revolution, while the states without excess land could not. Since all the states shared in the expense of the war, all should share in the bounty of the western land sales through the national government. Eventually, all the states agreed to this and the land outside the current boundaries was placed under the control of the national government.

The Land Ordinance. First of all, congress had to decide how to sell the land and what to do with the proceeds. These questions were answered with the Land Ordinance of 1785. The law required the land to be surveyed and divided for sale. It was divided into townships measuring six miles by six miles. The townships were further divided into thirty-six sections, each one square mile. The sixteenth section was sold to benefit public education. The money made from the sales was used to pay off the national debt.

Northwest Ordinance. The second decision Congress had to make, was how the land would be governed. Would the western lands be colonies for the east? Would they be subject to the control that Britain had once placed on America? These questions were answered for the Northwest and for all later U.S. territories by the Northwest Ordinance.

The Northwest Ordinance was a piece of legislation that was to have long-lasting effects in America. The Confederation Congress established the pattern that would be followed for over a hundred and fifty years of national expansion. The law required that new territories be under federal control until they had a population of 60,000. At that point, they could be admitted to the Confederation by Congress as a new state, having all the rights and privileges of the old ones. This farsighted piece of legislation ensured that America could grow with equal rights for citizens in newly added lands. America would be a free nation, not an empire.

Check the statements that were true of the Articles of Confederation.

3.1 _____ had a weak executive

3.2 _____ the states were sovereign

3.3 _____ Congress could not raise taxes

3.4 _____ it was only an alliance

3.5 _____ Congress could not declare war

3.6 _____ the national court system was weak

3.7 _____ the Congress could not pass any effective legislation

3.8 _____ Congress could handle Native Americans affairs

3.9 _____ commerce between the states was handled by Congress

3.10 _____ it was ratified in 1781

3.11 _____ it was the first government of the United States

3.12 _____ it was in effect for about twenty years

Complete these sentences.

3.13 The Confederation Congress passed the _____ to set up the government for the Northwest Territory.

3.14 All state land claims in the Northwest Territory were given to _____ .

3.15 Money made from land sales in the Old Northwest were used to pay _____ .

3.16 The Land Ordinance divided the Old Northwest into townships measuring _____ by _____ .

3.17 Townships, under the Land Ordinance, were divided into _____ sections of one square mile each and section _____ was sold to benefit public education.

3.18 A territory could be admitted as a state when the population reached _____ .

Problems under the Articles. The biggest problem facing the Confederation Congress in the 1780s, was the national economy. The nation had immense debts and no way of paying them. Congress could only request money from the states and it never got all it requested. Foreign nations did not trust American credit. Several of the states were printing money, freely causing widespread **inflation**.

Congress also could not regulate trade between the states and that was causing more problems. Several of the states were putting tariffs on goods from other states. Trade with foreign nations was regulated as each state saw fit. Some of the states set very low tariffs to attract foreign trade, while others set high ones to protect their own manufacturers.

There also was unrest among the people. The bad economy had put many people into debt. Debtors and creditors clashed. Several of the states, like Rhode Island, deliberately allowed inflation to help the debtors. (Inflation means money loses value and debts are paid back later with the less valuable currency. Or put another way, you pay back less than you borrowed.) The Revolution had encouraged rebellion over taxes as well as a disrespect for law and property. These attitudes were coming back to haunt the new government.

Annapolis Convention. The problems over commerce were substantial enough to call a meeting in Annapolis, Maryland in 1786 to deal with them. Only five states sent delegates. With such a poor showing, nothing could be done. But, Alexander Hamilton of New York managed to have the convention accept his recommendation for a meeting in Philadelphia the following year to revise the Articles. That meeting might have met the same fate except for an event in Massachusetts that frightened the states into action.

Shays' Rebellion. Massachusetts had not inflated its currency. In fact, that state had raised taxes and refused to help debtors. Farmers, many of them veterans from the Revolution, faced the loss of their farms due to personal debts or unpaid taxes. In 1786 the western part of the state erupted in rebellion under the leadership of Daniel Shays, a former Revolutionary soldier. The rebels demanded lower taxes, debt relief, and more paper money (inflation, also called cheap money).

Shays' Rebellion forced the closure of several courts to prevent foreclosures and imprisonment for debtors. The alarmed wealthy merchants of the east, who controlled the government, raised an army under General Benjamin Lincoln to quell the rebellion. He did so in early 1787 after several small skirmishes in which a few of the rebels were killed. Shays fled the state and was later pardoned.

Shays' Rebellion frightened the property owners and wealthy businessmen of the Confederation. These were the men in power in the state governments due to the property requirements to vote and hold office. They understood the threat Shays and others were to the process of law and government. They saw the need for a stronger national government to restore order and prevent mob rule. The Confederation Congress reluctantly approved the meeting called by the Annapolis Convention now scheduled for the summer of 1787 in Philadelphia. Its stated purpose was to revise the Articles of Confederation. It would do much more than that.

 Answer true or false.

If the statement is false, change some of the nouns or adjectives to make it true.

3.19 _____ Inflation helps creditors.

3.20 _____ The Annapolis Convention was called to discuss problems over state boundaries.

3.21 _____ Seven states sent delegates to the Annapolis Convention.

3.22 _____ The largest problem facing the Confederation Congress was the economy.

3.23 _____ Shays' Rebellion occurred in Massachusetts.

3.24 _____ Shays' Rebellion was put down by an army under the command of General Benjamin Lincoln.

3.25 _____ The poor people of the Confederation were frightened by Shays' Rebellion.

3.26 _____ America had good credit abroad under the Confederation.

3.27 _____ Some of the states put tariffs on goods from other states.

3.28 _____ States under the Confederation had the same tariffs on foreign goods.

Constitutional Convention

The meeting called for by the Annapolis Convention finally began on May 25, 1787 in the State House in Philadelphia. (It was later renamed Independence Hall). The fifty-five delegates came from twelve of the thirteen states. (Independent Rhode Island refused to participate). They were all well-to-do men chosen by the wealthy members of the state assemblies. The most radical leaders of the Revolution, such as Samuel Adams and Patrick Henry, were not there.

The men who did come were basically conservative, men who wanted a strong central government to prevent further rebellions. Among them were George Washington, Benjamin Franklin, James Madison (whose careful work earned him the title "Father of the Constitution"), Alexander Hamilton (a fierce advocate of a strong central government), and a host of lesser-known "Founding Fathers." Most of the delegates had served in the Revolution as either a soldier or administrator. They all understood the problems under the weak rule of Congress. Moreover, most had experience writing constitutions since all of the states had to write them after independence.

The delegates made several key decisions at the beginning. First of all, they elected George Washington as president of the convention. His immense prestige made him an obvious choice and gave the whole meeting a greater chance of success. The delegates also decided that their meetings would be completely secret. That enabled the men to debate and

| The delegates at the Constitutional Convention

compromise without being subject to outside pressure or having to explain their decisions before a final agreement was reached. (James Madison took detailed notes about the debates and decisions that were later published). Finally, the delegates decided not to revise the Articles, as they had been instructed. Instead, they decided to start over and write a whole new constitution. They had no authority to do this, but they felt that the Articles could not be amended to meet the country's needs.

Bundle of compromises. The Constitution of the United States was a bundle of compromises. The most important one involved the dispute over representation in Congress. The larger states supported the *Virginia Plan* which would have the states represented in Congress according to their population. This would give the more populous states more votes and the smaller states feared they would dominate the government. The smaller states, therefore, favored the *New Jersey Plan* in which each state had the same number of votes, no matter what its population. The larger states argued that they would pay more taxes without having any more representation.

This issue threatened to divide the convention and stop all progress on a constitution. Finally, an alternative, the *Connecticut Plan*, was proposed and approved. Under this plan, also called the *Great Compromise*, Congress was made up of two houses. Each state would have two representatives in the upper house, the Senate. But, the states would send representatives to the lower house, the House of Representatives, based on their population. Laws would have to pass both houses, so the Senate would protect the smaller states from being dominated by the larger. Also, laws involving money issues could only begin in the House of Representatives where the members more closely represented the percentage of taxes paid by each state. This compromise put the convention back on track.

Another issue the delegates had to face involved the counting of enslaved people. States in the South that had a larger number of slaves wanted them to be counted as part of the population to determine how many seats they got in the House of Representatives. Northern states wanted the enslaved people to count for taxation purposes. The compromise that was reached counted each slave as three-fifths of a person for both population and taxation purposes.

Most of the delegates wanted to end the slave trade (the importation of more Africans) because of the brutality it involved. But, several of the southern states would not accept giving Congress the authority to do that. By way of a compromise, Congress was denied that authority until the year 1807 (at which point it did end the trade). These were the key compromises of the Constitution.

Checks and balances. In their need to establish order and settle their own differences, the delegates did not forget they had just fought a war against a tyrannical government. They were determined not to create another one. Instead, they created a government in which power was divided among several branches, so that each would balance and check the others.

The power of government was divided between three branches of government: executive, legislative, and judicial. The executive, the president, could veto laws passed by Congress and appoint judges. The legislature, Congress, could override a veto, approve the appointment of judges and could **impeach** the president if he broke the law. The judiciary were judges appointed for life that could also be impeached by Congress and could declare a law unconstitutional (that is not expressly stated in the Constitution, but was assumed). Thus, each branch of the government had some control over the other. This division of power was a deliberate plan by the delegates to prevent any one person or part of the government from becoming too powerful.

The power of government was also divided between the states and the new federal government. The sovereignty of the states was kept. They simply lost certain powers to the national government. Any powers not specifically given to the national government were still kept by the states. For example, the states would run the police forces, set up schools, and handle many other local matters. But, the national government was given several key powers including the right to tax and to regulate commerce between the states.

The Results. The delegates at the Constitutional Convention debated in secrecy for almost four months. Finally, on September 17, 1787 they signed the final document. Of the original fifty-five delegates, only forty-two were still there. Three of those refused to sign it. The rest did and used their substantial means and prestige to have it ratified.

The delegates had acted without authorization when they wrote a new constitution. They did so again when they did not send the document to Congress, but to the states. Since Rhode Island had not even attended, they knew it was impossible to get all the states to ratify it. Therefore, the delegates agreed that it would go into effect as soon as nine of the thirteen states (two-thirds) had accepted it. This was also the basis for amending the Constitution.

The publication of the Constitution was a shock to the American public. They had been expecting some amendments to improve the Articles of Confederation. This was a completely new plan of government unlike any used before in history by a nation. It created a strong central government to replace the "union " of states. It raised fears of tyranny and taxation. The last major battle of the Revolution was to be fought over this document.

Answer these questions.

3.29 How many states were represented at the convention? _____

3.30 What social class did the delegates come from? _____

3.31 What three important decisions did the delegates make at the beginning of the convention?

   a. _____

   b. _____

   c. _____

3.32 What were the two proposals that were not accepted on representation in Congress? (Give the name of the plan and describe it.)

   a. _____

   b. _____

3.33 What was the other name of the Great Compromise? _____

3.34 What was the Great Compromise?

_____

_____

3.35 Why would the compromise on counting slaves be called the Three-Fifths Compromise?

_____

_____

3.36 What compromise was made on controlling the slave trade?

_____

3.37 What were the three branches of government power was divided between?

  a. _____   b. _____

  c. _____

3.38 What check did the

  a. executive have on the legislature?

  _____

  b. legislature have on the executive?

  _____

  c. judiciary have on the legislature and executive?

  _____

  d. executive have on the judiciary?

  _____

  e. legislature have on the judiciary?

  _____

3.39 What happened to the sovereignty of the states?

_____

_____

3.40 Did all of the delegates sign the Constitution? _____

3.41 How many states had to ratify the Constitution to put it into effect? _____

The Battle of Ratification

Battle Lines. The signing of the Constitution was followed by six months of heated public debate. The people that favored the document were called Federalists. Those that opposed it Anti-Federalists. Generally, the Federalists were from the wealthier classes. They were merchants who wanted a strong government to protect trade, property owners who feared lawlessness, and educated people who understood the problems of governing under the Articles. The Anti-Federalists were usually the poorer people, who feared that a strong central government might enforce payment of personal debts. These people distrusted governments of all sorts, especially strong ones. These were reinforced by the radicals of the Revolution. These people had fought for liberty from oppressive government and were not going to give it up now. Others believed in the independence of the states and did not want them to give up that much power to another government.

The Battle. The Federalists defended the Constitution in a whole storm of papers, speeches, articles, and essays. The most famous defense was the *The Federalist*, a series of essays originally published in New York and then in the other states. They were written by Alexander Hamilton, James Madison, and John Jay under the name *Publicus*. This brilliant analysis of the nature of republican government and the details of the Constitution was eventually put into book form and is still sold today.

The Anti-Federalists responded with attacks on the Constitution. They had one concern that drew the most attention. The Constitution did not protect the basic rights of the people. Many of the state constitutions included statements specifically protecting the right to trial by jury, freedom of speech, the right to petition the government and other important freedoms. Without these, the Anti-Federalists feared the people would have no protection from this

THE NEW NATION

Delaware
Pennsylvania
New Jersey
Georgia
Connecticut
Massachusetts
Maryland
South Carolina
New Hampshire
Virginia
New York
North Carolina
Rhode Island

The last two states to ratify were North Carolina and Rhode Island, both of which were notorious for being dedicated to individual rights and distrusting government.

NORTH CAROLINA
Ratified the Constitution:
November 1789

RHODE ISLAND
Ratified the Constitution:
May 1790

powerful new government. The Federalists agreed this was a valid consideration. They promised that the first order of business for the new Congress would be to pass amendments protecting the key freedoms of the people. (These were eventually passed and ratified as the Bill of Rights, the first ten amendments to the Constitution).

The Victory. The states called special conventions to vote on ratification beginning in the winter of 1787-88. The strong, well reasoned defense of the Federalists carried the day. The problems of the Articles of Confederation also drove many to accept the proposal. The promise of a Bill of Rights won over many others who opposed the new government.

Slowly the Federalists won over the necessary states. Delaware was the first state to ratify in December of 1787. Pennsylvania, New Jersey, Georgia, Connecticut, and Massachusetts followed that winter. In the spring, Maryland and South Carolina ratified it. The Constitution went into effect in June of 1788 when the ninth state, New Hampshire, approved it.

Two important states had not ratified the Constitution when it went into effect: Virginia, the first, largest, and most populous state, as well as the large, commercially important state of New York. Both of these states knew that the union was going to be formed with or without them. Realizing that they could not hope to prosper independent of the new order, both states ratified the Constitution in the summer of 1788. With these additions, the new government had enough support to make a solid start.

The two states that had still not ratified were North Carolina and Rhode Island, both of which were notorious for being dedicated to individual rights and distrusting government. Both finally realized they could not hope to go it alone in this case. But, North Carolina did not ratify the Constitution until November of 1789. Stubborn Rhode Island, which did not even send delegates to the convention, did not join the union until May of 1790, over a year after the first president took office.

In the end, all thirteen states approved the Constitution and created a powerful republic. The reasons why they did it were clearly spelled out in the document's preamble which states:

We the people of the United States, in order to form a more perfect union, establish justice, insure domestic tranquility, provide for the common defense, promote the general welfare, and secure the blessings of liberty to ourselves and our posterity, do ordain and establish this Constitution for the United States of America.

Preamble to The Constitution

The American Revolution (1763–1789) | Unit 3

Complete these sentences.

3.42 People who supported the Constitution were called _____ while opponents were called _____ .

3.43 The most serious objection to the Constitution was corrected with the passage of the _____ , the first ten amendments.

3.44 _____ was the first state to ratify the Constitution.

3.45 The Constitution went into effect after the state of _____ ratified it.

3.46 The two important states that had not ratified the Constitution when it went into effect were _____ and _____ .

3.47 The two states that did not ratify the Constitution until over a year after the others were _____ and _____ .

List the six reasons why the Constitution was written, according to the preamble.

3.48
1. _____
2. _____
3. _____
4. _____
5. _____
6. _____

Memorize the Preamble to the Constitution and recite it for your teacher.

TEACHER CHECK _____ _____
                  initials   date

Before you take this last Self Test, you may want to do one or more of these self checks.

1. _____ Read the objectives. See if you can do them.
2. _____ Restudy the material related to any objectives that you cannot do.
3. _____ Use the **SQ3R** study procedure to review the material:
    a. **S**can the sections.
    b. **Q**uestion yourself.
    c. **R**ead to answer your questions.
    d. **R**ecite the answers to yourself.
    e. **R**eview areas you did not understand.
4. _____ Review all vocabulary, activities, and Self Tests, writing a correct answer for every wrong answer.

SELF TEST 3

Match the following (each answer, 2 points).

3.01 _____ Articles of Confederation
3.02 _____ Northwest Ordinance
3.03 _____ Land Ordinance of 1785
3.04 _____ Annapolis Convention
3.05 _____ Shays' Rebellion
3.06 _____ Virginia Plan
3.07 _____ Great Compromise
3.08 _____ Bill of Rights
3.09 _____ *The Federalist*
3.010 _____ *Common Sense*

a. essays in favor of the Constitution
b. representation in Congress would be based on population
c. first ten amendments to Constitution
d. meeting of five states that called for the Constitutional Convention
e. representation by state in the Senate and by population in the House
f. Thomas Paine's essay that turned American opinion to independence
g. territory of 60,000 can be admitted as a state
h. Northwest divided into towns of 36 square miles for sale to pay off debt
i. America's first constitution
j. frightened many property owners to support the Constitution

Unit 3 | The American Revolution (1763–1789)

Name the person (each answer, 3 points).

3.011 _____ America's representative in France during the Revolution; played the "natural man," delegate to Constitutional Convention

3.012 _____ Commander-in-chief of American forces during the Revolution; president of the Constitutional Convention

3.013 _____ Author of the Declaration of Independence

3.014 _____ Father of the Constitution; took notes of the debate at the Constitutional Convention

3.015 _____ Hero at Ticonderoga and Saratoga; traitor at West Point

3.016 _____ American commander of southern army after Camden; lost all the battles; won the campaign

3.017 _____ French aristocrat; volunteer American soldier; American hero; gave his own money to the cause

3.018 _____ President of the Second Continental Congress; signed the Declaration of Independence in large letters

3.019 _____ Led a group of frontiersmen to capture British forts in the west, and 180 miles through waist-deep swamps to recapture Vincennes

3.020 _____ British commander in the south after the capture of Charleston; surrendered at Yorktown

Answer these questions (each answer, 4 points).

3.021 What battle was the turning point of the Revolutionary War?

_____

3.022 What were the three branches of government set up by the Constitution?

a. _____   b. _____

c. _____

3.023 How can the president check the power of Congress under the Constitution?

_____

3.024 How many states had to approve the Constitution before it went into effect?

_____

3.025 What was the economic theory used by the British to govern the colonies?

_____

3.026 What were the three American reactions to the Stamp Act?

a. _____   b. _____

c. _____

The American Revolution (1763–1789) | Unit 3

Answer true or false (each answer, 1 point).

3.027 _____ Rhode Island was the last of the thirteen states to ratify the Constitution.

3.028 _____ The Articles of Confederation did not allow Congress to raise taxes.

3.029 _____ The Confederation Congress could not declare war.

3.030 _____ The Constitution allowed enslaved people to count as one-third of a person for taxes and two-thirds for representation.

3.031 _____ The Constitution forbids Congress from ever regulating the slave trade.

3.032 _____ Under the Constitution, Congress can impeach the president for breaking the law.

3.033 _____ The Confederation Congress could regulate commerce between the states.

3.034 _____ Inflation helps debtors.

3.035 _____ Monmouth Courthouse was the last major battle in the North during the Revolutionary War.

3.036 _____ The Northwest Ordinance was passed by the Confederation Congress.

80/100 SCORE _____ TEACHER _____ _____
initials   date

Before taking the LIFEPAC Test, you may want to do one or more of these self checks.

1. _____ Read the objectives. See if you can do them.
2. _____ Restudy the material related to any objectives that you cannot do.
3. _____ Use the **SQ3R** study procedure to review the material.
4. _____ Review activities, Self Tests, and LIFEPAC vocabulary words.
5. _____ Restudy areas of weakness indicated by the last Self Test.

HISTORY & GEOGRAPHY 803

LIFEPAC TEST

NAME _____

DATE _____

SCORE _____

HISTORY & GEOGRAPHY 803: LIFEPAC TEST

Match these people (each answer, 2 points).

1. _____ Father of the Constitution
2. _____ Lost battles but won campaign in the South
3. _____ American general that turned traitor
4. _____ author of *Common Sense*
5. _____ president of the Constitutional Convention
6. _____ colonial representative in London right before the Revolution
7. _____ hanged as a spy during the New York campaign of 1776
8. _____ Boston radical, began Committees of Correspondence
9. _____ author of the Declaration of Independence
10. _____ American naval commander, *Bonhomme Richard*

a. George Washington
b. Benjamin Franklin
c. Nathanael Greene
d. Benedict Arnold
e. Samuel Adams
f. Thomas Jefferson
g. James Madison
h. John Paul Jones
i. Nathan Hale
j. Thomas Paine

Complete the following.

11. What was the Great Compromise of the Constitutional Convention? (5 points)

    _____
    _____
    _____

12. Describe the set up and results of the Battle of Yorktown. (5 points)

    _____
    _____
    _____

13. Why did British policy towards the colonies change after 1763? (5 points)

    _____
    _____
    _____

Unit 803 | **History & Geography**

14. Describe the most important provisions of each law (each answer, 2 points).

   Stamp Act: _____

   Quebec Act: _____

   Quartering Act: _____

   Townshend Acts: _____

   Intolerable Acts: _____

15. What was Shays Rebellion and why was it important? (5 points)

   _____

   _____

Complete each sentence using a word from the list (each answer, 2 points).

Lexington	Ticonderoga	Saratoga
Rochambeau	Monmouth	Camden
Trenton	Cornwallis	Lafayette
Steuben		

16. The Revolutionary War began at _____ .

17. The Marquis de _____ was a wealthy French volunteer who became an American hero.

18. _____ was the commander of the French army in America during the Revolution.

19. _____ was the indecisive last major battle in the North during the Revolution.

20. Lord _____ was the British commander in the South after the capture of Charleston.

21. Baron von _____ drilled the American army at Valley Forge.

22. Henry Knox dragged the cannon from _____ to Boston.

23. Horatio Gates lost the humiliating battle of _____ when he brought a new American army south after the loss of Charleston.

24. _____ was the turning point of the Revolutionary War.

25. Washington led his army across the icy Delaware River to surprise the Hessians at _____ on the day after Christmas.

LIFEPAC TEST | **3**

Name the legislature or constitution related to each item (each answer, 3 points).

26. _____ Declaration of Independence
27. _____ Stamp Act
28. _____ America's first constitution
29. _____ Northwest Ordinance
30. _____ enslaved people counted as three-fifths of a person
31. _____ America's first government
32. _____ reaction to the Intolerable Acts
33. _____ a firm league of friendship between the states
34. _____ checks and balances
35. _____ appointed Washington as commander-in-chief